Jerrold S. Parker
Herbert L. Waichman
Andres F. Alonso
Fred R. Rosenthal

Wiley Publishing, Inc.

Personal Injury Law For Dummies®

Published by
Wiley Publishing, Inc.
111 River Street
Hoboken, NJ 07030-5774
Copyright © 2009 by Wiley Publishing, Inc., Indianapolis, Indiana

Published by Wiley Publishing, Inc., Indianapolis, Indiana

Publisher's Acknowledgments

We're proud of this book; please send us your comments through our Dummies online registration form located at www.dummies.com/register/.

Some of the people who helped bring this book to market include the following:

Acquisitions, Editorial, and Media Development

Project Editor: Carrie A. Burchfield

Development Editor: Traci Cumbay

Business Development Representative: Melody Layne

Editorial Manager: Rev Mengle

Editorial Manager: Traci Cumbay

Custom Publishing Project Specialist: Michael Sullivan

Composition Services

Project Coordinator: Kristie Rees

Layout and Graphics: Reuben W. Davis, Melissa K. Jester

Proofreaders: Cindy Ballew, Jessica Kramer

Indexer: Broccoli Information Mgt.

Publishing and Editorial for Technology Dummies

    Richard Swadley, Vice President and Executive Group Publisher

    Andy Cummings, Vice President and Publisher

    Mary Bednarek, Executive Director, Acquisitions

    Mary C. Corder, Editorial Director

Publishing for Consumer Dummies

    Diane Graves Steele, Vice President and Publisher

Composition Services

    Gerry Fahey, Vice President of Production Services

    Debbie Stailey, Director of Composition Services

Table of Contents

Introduction

*W*e deal with all types of personal injury and wrongful death lawsuits every day, and so we know well the ins and outs of effectively handling these cases in order to achieve the best possible results for our clients. We are also well aware of the problems and pitfalls that arise and the steps that must be taken to deal with them effectively. In this book, we've used our combined experience and know-how to answer common questions and prepare readers to deal knowledgeably with any personal injury situation. We can't anticipate every question in a short book, but we do give you a basic working knowledge of the litigation process.

Although litigation may be the last thing on your mind when something terrible happens, the reality is that cases are often won or lost within a very small window of time immediately following an incident, as a result of the actions (or inaction) of the people involved in the event or by their attorneys. If you are injured, you need your team to be up and running without delay following the event, protecting your rights.

How This Book Is Organized

Chapters 1 to 3 give you general information about personal injury lawsuits, including working with an attorney and what to expect from the legal process.

In Chapters 4 through 10, you find specific information about each of several different types of situations and occurrences that may ultimately turn into a personal injury or wrongful death lawsuit.

Note: Although the summaries in Chapters 4 through 10 contain many steps that you should take in a given situation, no book can capture all possible scenarios and the summaries are merely instructive.

In order to help you use this book effectively, we also include a glossary, a list of statute of limitations by state and case type (Appendix A), and a directory of consumer protection agencies by state (Appendix B).

Icons Used in This Book

Here's a list of the icons you find in this book and what you can expect from the text they highlight.

Some information bears keeping in mind. We flag points you may want to return to again and again with this icon.

When we give you information that saves you time, money, or stress, this icon shows up next to it.

An idea or action that can cause you damage — physical, financial, emotional, or otherwise — is highlighted by this icon.

Chapter 1

Uncovering the Basics of Personal Injury Litigation

*I*f you're hurt as a result of the negligence or intentional act of a third party, unable to earn a living, and facing mounting medical expenses, the prospect of diving into a lawsuit can be intimidating. Before the moment actually comes, few people consider what they need to do immediately in such a situation. In this chapter, we explain what you need to know and do to get on the road to a fair award or settlement for your injuries.

This book is intended to be informational only and isn't offered as legal advice. Since the laws relating to personal injury actions vary from state to state and may change significantly based on acts of state legislatures, the federal government, and state and federal court decisions, you should always consult a qualified attorney with respect to any potential legal matter.

Understanding Personal Injury Litigation

In order for there to be a basis for any lawsuit, there must first be an injury (or death) that's caused by a third party's wrongful act, whether negligent or intentional. In addition, that third party must have breached some duty of care to the injured party; many accidents are simply nothing more than unfortunate occurrences caused by unforeseeable circumstances, emergency situations, natural disasters, freak occurrences, or some other event for which no one is responsible in the eyes of the law. In short, the injury must be a reasonably foreseeable result of the conduct that caused it. The only injuries for which compensation may be awarded are those which a reasonable person would view as a foreseeable consequence of the conduct upon which the lawsuit is based.

Personal injury and wrongful death lawsuits differ significantly in terms of the nature of the damages being sought. A personal injury action belongs only to the person who is injured or a spouse who suffers derivatively (as a direct result) of those injuries. Thus, in a personal injury action, the injured person is entitled to monetary damages for such things as conscious pain and suffering, lost earnings, and the loss of enjoyment of life, In a wrongful death action, a spouse's damages would include the value of the "loss of services" of the injured spouse such as the cost of replacing the services the injured husband or wife can no longer perform, including the loss of consortium (sexual relationship).

A wrongful death action, however, belongs to the estate of the deceased person, and the measure of damages is generally referred to as *the pecuniary loss to the distributees of the decedent* — a monetary figure to make up for what survivors of the deceased person have lost, including such things as the loss of inheritance, loss of services, loss of parental guidance, and other pecuniary (monetary) losses as well as funeral expenses.

All personal injury and wrongful death actions come about as the result of the negligent or intentional wrongful acts of a third party; however, that general categorization can then be broken down by case type. These include (and are explained in detail in the chapters to come)

- ✔ Transportation accidents of all kinds (motor vehicle, train, bus, plane, truck, ATV, tram, motorcycle, snowmobile, and so on)

- ✔ Premises accidents (snow and ice cases, stairway accidents, trip and fall cases, escalator and elevator accidents, and so on)

- ✔ Construction accidents

- ✔ Defective product cases (product liability)

- ✔ Defective pharmaceutical products

- ✔ Defective medical devices

- ✔ Toxic substances

- ✔ Municipal liability (sidewalk defects, municipal vehicles or employees involved, parks, schools, housing projects, subways, police, sanitation, and fire department cases, and so on)

- ✔ Professional malpractice (medical, dental, legal, accounting, engineering, brokerage, financial advisor, and so on)

- ✔ Nursing home cases

- ✔ Cases arising out of intentional acts (assault, battery, false imprisonment, malicious prosecution, libel, slander, and so on)

Taking Action As Soon As You're Hurt

We can't overemphasize the importance of taking immediate steps to protect your rights as soon as an injury occurs, whether you suspect it was caused by the negligent or intentional act of a third party or not. In fact, a case can be lost even before an injured person retains an attorney as a result of ill-advised statements to third parties, lost evidence, the failure to take photographs or get the names of witnesses, refusing medical care, or any number of other oversights.

Although these important steps are somewhat similar regardless of the type of case involved, there are several significant differences as well. Each chapter provides a list to review so that if you're involved in an accident or other incident, you're better able to respond in a way that maximizes your chance for a favorable outcome.

Keeping records

The more details you have about your injury, the better off you are in a trial. Start keeping records even before you see an attorney. You need to keep a diary of

- ✔ Your medical visits and procedures, including the reasons for them, diagnoses made, medications prescribed, out-of-pocket costs, and so on

- ✔ Any pain, inabilities, limitations, days out of work, and other similar items

- ✔ How you feel on a daily basis — any improvement or deterioration in your condition

- ✔ Conversations with anyone concerning any aspect of the case

- ✔ Anything you remember about the incident

You also need to collect records such as the following:

- ✔ Bills related to the case, such as those for transportation, medical, and pharmacy expenses

- ✔ Documents that indicate all doctors' names, addresses, telephone numbers, and specialties

- ✔ Relevant photographs (those showing your injury, disability, healing, and so on)

- ✔ Letters regarding insurance, disability, or Workers' Compensation

- ✔ Any legal papers you may receive or be served with

- ✔ Names and addresses of witnesses

After you've made a copy of these things, turn the originals over to your attorney immediately. Always keep a copy of everything you give to your attorney.

Getting medical (and other) care

Although it seems to be a contradiction, many injured parties (plaintiffs) are somewhat less than diligent in getting necessary medical care, keeping up with their physical rehabilitation, or taking their medications as directed. Those folks who are injured also very often refuse to go for psychological or psychiatric counseling. In general, people just don't want to think of themselves or appear to others as a complainer or sick person.

If you need medical treatment or care, don't hesitate to get it. If you have a problem paying for it, your attorney may be able to help by having medical providers take a *lien* (a legal claim) against the proceeds of your case so that you can receive the treatment you need including surgery and rehabilitation. This lien is part of the medical expenses you incurred because of the accident and should be considered an additional element of damages to be paid by the proceeds of any settlement or award.

Many jurisdictions provide social services of various types by taking liens against the proceeds of your case if you're successful.

Many states also have no-fault insurance for automobile accident cases that provides for payment of your medical and hospital bills if certain conditions are met, regardless of whose fault the accident was. You may also qualify for certain state-run disability programs or other similar plans that pay you in the event of a hit-and-run accident or one in which the defendant has no automobile insurance.

You can obtain coverage for needed medical care as a result of an accident in many different ways. Cost generally should not be a factor. Getting better is the goal, and most of the time, that requires the care of competent healthcare providers.

Lapses in medical care, failure to follow up on rehabilitation, not taking prescribed medications, or not obtaining professional counseling makes it appear that an injury isn't as severe as you claim it is or that it doesn't have any psychological impact on your life. These situations often have a significant negative impact on the result in a personal injury case.

Don't expect your attorney to give medical advice. Your attorney will advise you about the significance proper and full medical care has on your case and even assist you in finding an appropriate medical professional. You, however, must take charge of your medical care and pursue it in a way that not only helps you recover as completely as possible but also makes your case a solid one.

Remaining on your guard

Because personal injury litigation involves the potential for the parties being sued (the defendants) to be liable for substantial damage awards, they and their insurance carriers make every effort to defeat your claim or reduce its value. Defense counsels and insurance companies regard litigation as a high-stakes poker game where anything goes in terms of protecting the defendant and the insurer's money.

Keep in mind the following tips, which assist you and your attorney in obtaining the best results possible:

- Don't speak to anyone about the occurrence or your injuries, especially representatives from defendant's insurance company or their investigators. These people aren't your friends, and they're not there to help you. Their only goal is to save the defendant and insurance company money.

  Refrain from discussing incidents with your neighbors, friends, and relatives. Often the insurance companies send investigators to interview these people and may take depositions from them as litigation proceeds.

- If you're involved in an automobile accident with your own car, you may actually become involved in two separate law suits. You may bring a case against another driver (or owner) for injuries you have suffered; however, you may also be sued and become a defendant in a case brought against you by one of your passengers, a pedestrian, or the driver (or passenger) in the other vehicle.

  You must retain your own attorney to handle a case you bring as a result of your injuries; however, your insurance company must provide (and pay for) an attorney to defend you with respect to claims made against you. Between the two attorneys, you're fully protected and properly represented on both sides of the case.

- Be aware that as the potential value of a case increases, so does the allocation of resources and personnel by the defendant's insurance company. Even in smaller cases, a defense investigator is assigned to interview witnesses, take photographs, and gather evidence. In significant cases, however, several investigators may be assigned to follow you, videotape you doing anything that may be inconsistent with your injury claims, and even set up staged situations to see how you react. In our experience, the jury generally doesn't believe you when you testify that you put on a spare tire, for instance, while in terrible pain.

✔ Surveillance activity increases as your trial date gets closer.

✔ You may always talk to the police, but be aware that they sometimes make mistakes in recording information if it's not presented clearly. Always be sure that the officer you're speaking to gets the story straight.

✔ You should always talk to your doctors and hospital employees. Just remember to be sure to let them know what your complaints are. You can't expect a jury to sympathize with your situation if you keep telling your doctor or nurses, "I'm fine" or "the pain isn't that bad," when you're really in agony.

✔ Don't sign any documents (except for those from or approved by your attorney) without reading them thoroughly and understanding what they mean. If you must sign something, be sure to get a copy of it when you sign it. The best practice is to have your attorney review any document you're asked to sign.

✔ Don't divulge information over the Internet in blog postings or on social networking sites like MySpace and Facebook. Public sites are just that — public. Comments you make about your motivations or injuries are there for the world to see or for defense counsel to obtain directly or through discovery requests.

✔ Posting photographs or videos may make you appear to be less injured than you claim or certainly not as emotionally distraught as you represent. Video from your wedding or that of one of your children or relatives that took place two weeks after the accident showing you doing the limbo will be greatly appreciated by the defense attorney. Insurance companies search the Web for these videos. You may simply be making the best of an important family event while in terrible pain, but a jury is unlikely to see it that way.

Hiring an Attorney

Some people believe that you need to hire an attorney only in the most complicated personal injury cases, or where catastrophic injuries or death is involved. Simply stated, that's a very serious error.

The old adage that someone who tries to represent himself in a criminal case "has a fool for a client and an idiot for a lawyer" applies to any civil personal injury case, too. Over the past 50 years, the law has matured, becoming highly complex and requiring specialized professional knowledge. The legislative and judicial systems of each state and the federal government have enacted so many new laws and handed down so many interpretations of those laws (as well as of existing laws that required reanalysis in light of changes in society, technology, and the economy) that most attorneys now limit their practice to just one or a few areas of civil law. Well-financed attorneys hired by insurance companies to represent defendants therefore are well-prepared and better equipped than ever.

A plaintiffs' attorney normally gets paid only if he brings a case to a successful conclusion by recovering money in a settlement or after a trial. Defense firms bill their clients (the insurance companies) by the hour for everything they do, and collect their fees whether they win or lose your case. Therefore, defense firms have an incentive to delay your case and litigate it for as long as possible.

In certain situations, your attorney may seek an "of counsel" relationship with an attorney who specializes in a particular type of case, such as product liability, defective pharmaceuticals, defective medical devices, toxic torts, nursing home abuse, medical malpractice, consumer fraud, or mass torts. This common practice is designed to make certain that you are represented by an attorney who is best qualified to handle your particular type of case. You have a right to approve or disapprove of the "of counsel" attorney.

Represent yourself, and you're likely to run into a settlement proposal from a defense attorney who smells your inexperience and is taking advantage of your knowledge gap about the medical and financial benefits you may be entitled to.

Unfortunately, after settlements are agreed on and money is paid to the injured person, very little, if anything can be done to fix the mistake.

Because an unrepresented, injured person often needs money immediately, any settlement she agrees to may be the product of desperation without considering such things as future lost earnings, future medical expenses, and the very real possibility of the injury being much more serious than it first seemed to be. Often, the full extent of an injury doesn't materialize until months after the incident — when the ink has long since dried on a settlement and the injured person has no further options.

An experienced attorney with an established track record of success may be very familiar to defense attorneys and insurance companies, who recognize that attorneys know the value of the case and that they can't take any unfair advantage of you. This fact alone may lead to a more favorable settlement. An experienced attorney also takes all immediate steps necessary to protect a client, so if a settlement doesn't take place, no rights are lost through the failure to hire an investigator, interview a witness, hire an expert, or preserve evidence.

Retaining an attorney is your first priority in any situation involving an injury or death, or any type of professional malpractice involving personal injury and monetary damages. Insurance company studies have shown that people who hire an attorney receive, on average, three times more money than people who do not hire an attorney and settle their cases on their own.

Selecting the right attorney

Checking the Yellow Pages or writing down a phone number from a TV ad aren't the most reliable ways to find the best attorney for your particular situation. You do have several better avenues for choosing an attorney, including the following:

- ✔ Asking for recommendations from friends or family members who've had favorable experiences with their attorneys

> ✔ Contacting local bar associations, which maintain lists of attorneys specializing in various areas of the law
>
> ✔ Consulting Web sites and bona fide private organizations that rate attorneys in various categories based on peer reviews from other attorneys and judges
>
> One great example is the almost 100-year-old Martindale-Hubbell Law Directory: `www.martindale.com`.
>
> ✔ Asking for referrals from another attorney you may have used in the past for a different type of legal matter
>
> ✔ Contacting attorneys and law firms with a track record of having successfully represented clients with similar legal problems
>
> Research these attorneys online by searching for news articles and other publicity on high-profile cases, which always mention the names of the attorneys or law firms involved.
>
> ✔ Asking your employer, union representative, or insurance broker for the names of attorneys or law firms with the right expertise
>
> Many companies, unions, and brokers maintain extensive lists of attorneys specifically to assist their employees, members, and customers when they need legal help.

As you work to select an attorney, ask for consultations with those people you're interested in hiring. You may need more than one consultation with the same attorney or separate consultations with several attorneys before you find someone you believe is knowledgeable and experienced and with whom you feel comfortable working.

Remember, your attorney works for you and only you, and in many cases, the association may last for several years. Like most personal relationships, the one between an attorney and his client is built on trust and has its ups and downs. Being comfortable with your decision is therefore critical to reaching a satisfactory conclusion.

Retaining an attorney

Selecting an attorney and actually retaining one are two entirely different matters. When you finally retain an attorney, you enter into a contract that clearly defines all of the duties of the attorney as well as the legal fee you will be responsible for if you are successful in recovering by way of a settlement or judgment after trial. The terms of the retainer are standard (although they vary from state to state) and are fixed by state law.

While it is extremely important to retain an attorney as quickly as possible after an injury or death, you should never feel as though you are being rushed into signing anything, especially a *retainer agreement,* which is a contract between a client and an attorney. You must fully understand everything you're being told and be comfortable with what you're signing.

Retainers vary significantly from state to state, with respect to different types of cases in the same state (negligence, medical malpractice, federal tort claims), and sometimes even depending on the degree to which a case must be prosecuted (for example, if a settlement occurs in the pretrial stage, during trial, after an appeal, and so on). Cases involving injured children or wrongful death often require final court approval of any settlement as well as approval of the amount of the attorneys' fees and expenses claimed by the attorney. The terms of all retainers in personal injury and wrongful death cases are often dictated by rules enacted by each state's legislature, judiciary, or other regulatory agency. Attorneys must strictly follow their state's guidelines and aren't permitted to create their own terms and conditions in their retainers.

Many advertisements for attorneys make it appear as if they're giving their clients a benefit that other attorneys don't. For example, a law firm may advertise as follows: "You pay nothing unless we're successful and obtain money for your case." That type of statement, while true, is misleading. All states require a *contingent fee retainer* for personal injury and wrongful death cases, under which no client pays an attorney's fee unless the attorney is, in fact, successful in recovering money for the client. Some states require that the client remains responsible for the case expenses regardless of the outcome to avoid the potential of attorney's making a gift to a potential client.

Contingent fee retainers (as opposed to civil or criminal retainers, where the plaintiff must pay an agreed upfront amount, a fixed hourly rate, or an agreed lump sum regardless of the outcome of the case) are the foundation of the personal injury litigation field. Without this type of retainer agreement, few, if any, clients would have the financial resources to pay ongoing attorneys' fees during the course of a lawsuit and would therefore miss out on critical legal representation.

The contingent fee system discourages frivolous litigation by making attorneys more cautious about which cases they accept because they won't get paid if they lose the case. (Frivolous cases are almost always lost.) The contingent fee retainer system also ensures that attorneys work harder for their clients, because they know they get no fee if they lose the case.

Case expenses (sometimes referred to as *case disbursements*) cover such things as court filing fees, out-of-pocket expenses such as carfare and meals that are directly related to the case, copies of medical records, postage, expert fees, and so on. You need to discuss expenses with your attorney before you sign a contingent fee retainer and be certain that you understand whether you will be responsible for them. Attorneys aren't usually permitted to finance their client's cases or lend money to their clients during the course of litigation. Such conduct is referred to as *champerty* — an unethical investment by an attorney in his client's lawsuit.

Expenses and disbursements can add up to thousands of dollars in the average case and tens of thousands of dollars in more complex cases (like medical malpractice and products liability cases) that require the retention of highly specialized experts. Sometimes, expenses may even be measured in the hundreds of thousands, or millions, of dollars, as in pharmaceutical and medical device cases, class actions, and mass tort cases. Clearly, if a client was expected to pay such expenses as they came due, most lawsuits would fail before proceeding very far.

Most people would never even retain an attorney knowing that they couldn't afford to finance the litigation out-of-pocket expenses, and therefore the law permits an attorney to advance payment for case-related expenses and disbursements. Whether the client remains responsible for the payment of the case expenses advanced by the attorney depends on state rules and the terms of the retainer agreement. In any event, the attorney advances the payment of all expenses and disbursements, which are deducted from the plaintiff's recovery if the case is successfully resolved.

In some jurisdictions the expenses are paid back to the attorney in full and deducted from the client's share of the recovery, while in other jurisdictions, the expenses are shared by the plaintiff and the attorney in some proportion, often controlled by the retainer agreement and state rules. Even if the client remains responsible for case expenses when the case is unsuccessful, in reality, an attorney rarely seeks payment of the expenses and disbursements from the client.

In cases in which a person is seriously injured and hospitalized or is convalescing in a rehabilitation facility or at home, an attorney (or a representative or investigator) may visit that person to discuss the case and obtain a signed retainer. Be very wary of any attorney who, uninvited, approaches you (personally or through an investigator or other agent) before you make contact with the attorney. Soliciting clients is almost universally not permitted and violates state law. Attorneys who do approach you before you make contact with an attorney are the ones who gave rise to the phrase "ambulance chasers" or "runners." They give the legal profession a bad name and certainly don't represent the vast majority of ethical attorneys who follow the rules of ethics.

Chapter 2

Knowing What to Expect from Your Lawsuit

Although many people are familiar with the term *litigation,* most find that being involved in a lawsuit is a mysterious journey into the unknown. Peculiar procedures, strange rules, and unusual language are just some of the things the average person may find confusing or intimidating about filing a lawsuit. This chapter takes you through what you can expect from personal injury litigation.

Telling the Whole Truth during Intake and Investigation

One of the most important stages of any case is the *intake and investigation phase,* during which you are expected to tell your attorney and his investigators and experts exactly what happened to you and under what circumstances. Many significant cases are won or lost during this phase.

Don't try to make your case sound better than it is by misleading your attorney or his investigator. Such conduct jeopardizes your relationship with your attorney and comes back to haunt you when defense counsels and their investigators uncover inconsistencies in your story.

The sooner you retain an attorney, the quicker work can begin on the case and, generally, the greater likelihood of success. After you retain an attorney, immediately turn over everything you have that has any relevance to the case. (We give you a rundown of common records you need in Chapter 1.) You also need to tell your attorney everything you possibly can about the incident — the good, the not-so-good, the bad, and even the ugly.

Your attorney can fully protect your rights only if he knows everything possible about the case. Surprises destroy even great cases and always make the person who withheld information look like a liar — or at least like she was hiding the information. Rest assured, the insurance company's attorney *will* discover all the details you want to hide.

Don't withhold any information, no matter how embarrassing it may be; everything you tell your attorney is protected by the attorney-client privilege. You may not like it, but when you bring a lawsuit, the defendant is entitled to any information that affects your claim or credibility in a negative way.

After you retain an attorney, many things occur before a lawsuit is actually started. These include

- Dispatching one or more investigators to go to the scene of the accident to take photographs and measurements, gather important information, such as witness statements, and interview police officers who responded to the accident scene

- Sending claim letters to the potential defendants (and their insurance companies, if known) to immediately put them on notice of the occurrence

- Obtaining police reports, medical records, accident reports, Freedom of Information Act (FOIA) requests, no-fault claim forms, medical authorizations, and so on

- Retaining experienced experts, if the case warrants, to conduct inspections and tests, review medical records and reports, perform accident reconstruction work or create computer simulations, consult in numerous scientific areas when the case involves such things as

> pharmaceuticals, medical devices, and over-the-counter (OTC) drug products, analyze weather data, or offer opinions about what needs to be done to prove your case

✔ Obtaining all relevant medical records

✔ Exploring settlement possibilities and discussions with the defendant's insurance company

What to Expect after Litigation Begins

After a lawsuit is started, you may begin to appreciate the complexity of the judicial process and why you need a trusting attorney to guide you through. Litigation isn't for the faint of heart nor is it for attorneys without the proper expertise in your kind of case. You must heed your attorney's advice, refrain from doing anything you're told not to do, and most importantly, take the matter very seriously. Always be prepared to meet with your attorney when necessary and be available for court appearances.

Don't put off important events like depositions or physical examinations. Judges don't appreciate litigants who procrastinate, delay the smooth progress of a lawsuit, or disrupt the orderly flow of the court's business.

Always keep in touch with your attorney. Law firms have hundreds or even thousands of cases, so they usually contact clients only when necessary. Often, your personal involvement isn't necessary even though a lot may be going on behind the scenes. You have a right to ask about the progress of your case whenever you like. But be sure your attorney has your current contact information including your cell phone number and e-mail address and the contact information of at least one or two family members, friends, or neighbors who always know how to reach you immediately.

Understanding insurance

Insurance coverage may come from policies the defendant has or from insurance you've purchased. Many people don't realize that they have their own insurance that covers them

for injuries sustained in an incident caused by another
person.

The defendant (which may turn out to be you if you're sued
for an accident in your home or one involving your automobile, for example) may have various types of insurance:

- ✔ **Primary insurance** consists of basic policies, such as
  automobile, homeowners, apartment, fire, business
  premises, commercial vehicle, and general liability.

- ✔ **Excess insurance** refers to a policy that pays out its
  coverage after the primary coverage is exhausted. Excess
  coverage may have different layers, each of which
  pays out only when the entire coverage is exhausted. If
  the different types of policies are written by different
  insurance companies, each may have its own attorney.

- ✔ **Umbrella insurance** is usually sold to individuals as
  opposed to businesses and covers losses over and above
  the coverage of one or more primary or excess policies.
  An umbrella policy may be purchased to provide protection over many primary policies at the same time (automobile, home, apartment, boat, aircraft, and so on).

- ✔ **Comprehensive insurance** is coverage you buy to pay
  for damage to your vehicle as soon as it occurs. This
  insurance covers claims such as accidents, fires, theft,
  and broken glass. Your insurance company pays you
  immediately and then goes after the responsible party.
  Comprehensive insurance can be expensive but also
  allows you to have your car fixed or replaced long before
  a lawsuit is resolved.

- ✔ **Underinsurance** is automobile insurance that covers
  you in situations where the defendant has inadequate
  insurance to cover the personal injury damage caused
  to you. After the defendant's coverage is exhausted,
  your company pays you for your additional losses up to
  the limits of your underinsured policy.

- ✔ **Uninsured coverage** is automobile insurance that covers
  you in situations where the defendant has no insurance
  at all.

- ✔ **No-fault insurance** pays a carrier for medical costs, lost
  wages, and other expenses regardless of whether he was
  the one responsible for an accident. In no-fault states,
  litigation is reduced by having the injured party's insurer

pay the out-of-pocket expenses in smaller cases where lawsuits against the defendant are permitted. If your injuries don't meet the threshold for litigation, then you generally can't file a lawsuit to recover damages, even for pain and suffering, no matter how badly the defendant was at fault for the accident.

In many states, what is and isn't a threshold injury has been carefully defined by courts through litigation and can't be found by merely reading the statute. This reason is why you should have an experienced personal injury attorney advising you.

Many states allow you to stack various types of policies to obtain maximum coverage. Most states also have state-funded programs that provide coverage to people injured in hit-and-run automobile accidents or when the responsible party has no insurance at all. If you can afford it, stacking automobile polices is often a good idea.

Knowing What Happens After a Lawsuit Is Underway

In many jurisdictions, an action begins when a complaint is filed with the appropriate court authority, such as the county clerk or the clerk of the court. However, in several jurisdictions an action is started when a complaint is served on the defendant by a process server, sheriff, marshal, or some other person permitted by law to serve complaints in a particular state and then filed with the appropriate court authority.

Whether a case is filed as an individual claim or grouped with other similar claims is determined on a case-by-case basis. A *complaint* (or *pleading*) is usually the first document in a lawsuit and is designed to give the defendant specific information about why, where (in which court), and for how much she is being sued. (However, some jurisdictions have rules for when you can and can't claim a specific monetary amount in a complaint.)

The complaint gives some detail about what happened to the plaintiff or plaintiffs, when the occurrence took place, and what the defendant is accused of having done wrong. Different attorneys have different views about how much information they want to plead. Some give a minimal amount of information and some use the complaint as a discovery device to gain information from the defendant at a very early stage of the litigation through the responses defendants are required to give to each allegation in the complaint.

In certain cases, the true plaintiff isn't able or permitted to bring a lawsuit. These situations involve infants, death actions, and those where the injured party is mentally incompetent to protect his rights. In these cases, the court often appoints a legal representative (a guardian or administrator) for the injured or deceased party. When an infant is involved, one of the parents usually is the guardian in the lawsuit.

In most jurisdictions, whenever a case is brought by the legal representative for another person, any settlement or other resolution of the case must be formally approved by the court, which often determines the amount of the legal fee and approves the case-related expenses being claimed.

When a Notice of Claim is required

When a state, a *municipality* (the federal government, a state, city, county, town, and so on, or a unit within those divisions, like a school district, parks department, or public hospital) is going to be a defendant in a civil action, most jurisdictions require some form of early notice to be filed as a condition precedent to the start of the lawsuit.

These notices must set forth all the essential information in sufficient detail. Otherwise, your notice may be deemed insufficient by a court at a later date, and you will forever lose your right to bring a lawsuit. Further, the notice almost always has to be filed within a relatively short time after the occurrence, often within as little as 30, 60, or 90 days. Failure to file a timely, proper, and adequately pled Notice of Claim could end your case before it ever gets started. (Some exceptions exist if the claimant is an infant, an incompetent or is hospitalized, but without an acceptable excuse, you could be looking at a dismissal of your claim.) Many states do provide for a late Notice of Claim to be filed but only with court approval and for a good reason. Don't take chances.

Examining Special Case Types

You most likely will file a case with one defendant and one plaintiff, but you may also be part of a case that involves several other defendants or plaintiffs. We tell you about those kinds of cases in these sections.

Class actions

Sometimes a defendant or group of defendants causes financial harm (for example, consumer class actions involving a product that, because of a defect, is worthless but not dangerous) or personal injuries to a large group of potential plaintiffs. Although the class of potential plaintiffs may be identifiable (all purchasers of a particular year and model of a motor vehicle, for example, or all clients of a certain accounting firm), locating all members of the class and having them take part in an orderly litigation may be difficult or impossible.

As a result, a class action lawsuit is filed by one or more plaintiffs on behalf of themselves and the larger group of people "who are similarly situated." The court must find that the claims of the class members contain questions of law or fact in common before the lawsuit can proceed as a class action. The court then selects a limited number of attorneys or law firms to act in a coordinated fashion in a plaintiff's steering committee as counsel to the class. By trying issues common to all members of the class in one trial, a single judge is able to hear all the cases at the same time, with the resulting decision binding on all parties.

If, however, the court finds the proof needed to support the plaintiffs' claims or their measure of damages varies, the class isn't certified, and the individual plaintiffs are left to proceed on their own. Because the type, level, and amount of damages for each person in a class for a personal injury case necessarily vary, personal injury cases are rarely permitted to proceed as a class action.

Class action litigation is complex and time consuming, and any attorney or law firm selected to serve as class counsel must have considerable expertise in the area of class action litigation, the ability to fund the litigation and retain numerous experts if necessary, and the confidence of the court that the class is competently represented by class counsel.

Mass tort litigation

A *mass tort* is a civil case involving numerous injured plaintiffs and one or a few defendants, usually for cases involving injury or disease from catastrophic events, pharmaceutical products, medical devices, or toxic substances. In the federal system, these cases are coordinated before a single federal judge, usually with the assistance of a small group of special masters and experts, for the stated purpose of managing pre-trial discovery. In almost all cases, that federal judge ends up resolving the issue nationally, often in coordination with numerous state court judges, who have state court cases pending before them.

Mass tort cases differ from class actions in that each mass tort plaintiff generally has her own individual case. That case is consolidated with hundreds or thousands of other individual cases but retains, at all times, its own identity.

Because of the common issues and actors, the aggregate value of all claims in the same mass tort rises and falls on the outcomes of individual cases or with other decisive developments. Thousands of cases might be resolved as a result of a single negotiated agreement or trial outcome. Moreover, given the extremely high cost of litigation, coordinated mass tort litigation provides a legal forum to plaintiffs who might otherwise be unable to proceed on their own due to financial constraints of funding a single case.

Mass tort litigation does present difficulties, however, including

- Factual and legal issues raised by *latent* (dormant) injuries

- Problems that future injuries and future plaintiffs pose for settlement efforts

- Typical conflicts of interest posed by collective litigation

- The predicament courts face when attempting to aggregate cases

> Safeguards have been successfully employed in this regard. Courts often appoint *Special Masters* to oversee the settlement of mass tort cases especially when there's an aggregate settlement. The Special Master establishes protocols, procedures, and safeguards to ensure that only individuals who actually fall into the settlement matrix are compensated and that similarly situated individuals are compensated to a similar degree.

Mass tort litigation presents the justice system with unique challenges, which courts and attorneys have responded to with numerous procedural innovations. Clearly, this type of litigation is well beyond the capabilities of the average law firm. The specialized expertise needed to competently represent plaintiffs involved in a mass tort case, coupled with the significant financial and personnel demands generated by discovery and the need to retain highly qualified experts, effectively eliminates all but the most elite plaintiffs' attorneys and law firms from getting involved in a leadership role in this type of litigation.

Market share liability

Market share liability is a type of litigation that allows recoveries in situations where the plaintiffs have no idea which defendant actually caused their injuries, but one of an identifiable group of defendants certainly is responsible.

Market share liability was devised in the early 1980s in order to permit recovery by the victims of the generic miscarriage preventative diethylstilbestrol (DES). Some 4.8 million pregnant women took between 1938 and 1971. Many daughters of those women later developed a rare form of vaginal cancer, and in 1971 the FDA banned the drug's use. It was impossible for most of the injured women to identify the actual company that manufactured the specific drug their mothers were prescribed.

In a landmark case, the California Supreme Court fashioned a way in which to preserve the plaintiffs' right to recover by apportioning liability among all DES manufacturers according to their individual share of the entire DES market. Thus, each plaintiff recovered some amount from each defendant.

After the DES precedent was set, victims of other defective products urged courts to extend market share liability. Most of these efforts failed, however, because the other products were not as completely interchangeable as the generic drug DES.

Market share liability was not used for some twenty years, when the Wisconsin Supreme Court permitted a victim of childhood lead poisoning to proceed to trial under Wisconsin's variation of market share liability.

Creative approaches to protecting the rights of injured parties, like market share liability, are what separate ordinary attorneys from the ones who continue to forge new boundaries in civil tort law.

Serving the Answer

The *answer* is a document served by the defendant on the plaintiff in which the defendant has to answer each allegation contained in the plaintiff's complaint. The defendant may deny or admit to allegations, or the defendant can deny knowledge or information sufficient to respond with a denial or an admission.

When the answer is served, *issue is joined,* and the case can then proceed. Each defendant must serve her own answer. Usually, the defendant also serves many other documents with the answer. (The upcoming "Discovery" section tells you more.)

The first court conference

In most jurisdictions, after the two sides have started litigating a case, the court gets involved in order to move things along and avoid delays. At an initial conference, the parties usually fill out various forms and make certain demands for information on each other, or the court may use the various discovery documents already served on each other by the parties. Often, the courts have standard discovery schedules that must be completed within a specific time period before or after the initial conference.

The court may also decide specific issues that can't be agreed on by the attorneys. A schedule is usually set for compliance with discovery demands, the taking of *depositions* (examinations before trial), and the setting of a trial date or date in which the case is trial ready. Although your attorney may advise you of the conference, you aren't required to attend this (and most other) preliminary court appearances.

Discovery

Discovery (also called *disclosure*) is the process by which each party in a civil action learns about the evidence (documentary, testimonial, identification of witnesses, and so on) that the other side plans to use at trial. This process makes litigation more orderly and avoids surprises at trial. It also promotes settlements and enables the court to make determinations regarding the merits of the plantiff's case and the viability of the defense's case. Some initial discovery demands seeking specific information from the plaintiff are usually served with the defendant's answer.

In some states, *interrogatories* — questions for the plaintiff to answer — may be served. These questions may take the place of a *bill of particulars* (a document served by the plaintiff that supplies specific information regarding the otherwise broad and general allegations contained in the complaint) or deposition in certain jurisdictions. Requests for medical and lost wage authorizations are routinely requested, if not required, by automatic discovery rules.

All discovery or disclosure is designed to clarify the issues involved, let each side have as much information as possible about the other side's case (to avoid "trial by ambush"), and to make the trial proceed more smoothly when and if it takes place. It comes in two flavors:

- ✔ **Paper discovery** refers to the production of records, statements, names and addresses, authorizations to obtain medical records or other personal information, evidence of similar occurrences in the past (within limits set by the court), and other materials and information required by each side in preparation for trial or to more accurately evaluate the liability or damage aspects of the case.

> ✔ **Oral depositions** are taken under oath and recorded by a court reporter, and a growing number are even video-taped. Giving a deposition is the equivalent of testifying at trial before the court and jury. Each side is entitled to depose the other, and the questioning can go on for hours or even days. Unlike in a criminal case, however, the defendant in a civil case must testify and cannot invoke the Fifth Amendment to escape doing so. The plaintiff must testify unless unable to do so for a reason the court accepts. The plaintiff is usually deposed first, followed by the defendant.

Sometimes, more than one witness testifies for one or both sides. Thus, a husband and wife or a parent and child may testify for the plaintiff. When a defendant is a company, people must testify on its behalf. Accordingly, one witness is often an officer or other managerial-level employee and another may be an employee who was present when the accident occurred or who has special knowledge of the event.

Witnesses may also be questioned under oath to see what they know about the matter. In several jurisdictions, each side's treating doctors and expert witnesses may also be examined at a deposition in order to see the exact nature of their opinions and on what they're based.

Your attorney prepares you for your deposition so you're ready to answer questions truthfully and intelligently. You're there to tell the truth and not to spin the facts. You're instructed not to give too much information by rambling on and on, going beyond the question asked, guessing, or making things up because you don't remember something. Short, truthful answers are best; stick to *yes* and *no* whenever possible. If you truly don't remember something, say so immediately. "I don't remember" is an excellent answer, if it's true.

You may be shown documents or photographs at your deposition to confirm what they are, identify them, or vouch for their accuracy. These pieces of physical evidence are marked as exhibits and are then preserved for possible use at trial.

After you testify, you receive a copy of the transcript, which you can review and change if necessary to correct errors, fill in blanks, or clarify information.

When you bring a lawsuit against an individual, company, or municipality, you place much of your personal history in the limelight. Your prior medical, criminal, employment, and family history are all investigated. Because this information may have a bearing on your credibility, the extent of your monetary damages, or your claim for physical or psychological injuries, the defendant is entitled to ask you about it at your deposition or in interrogatories. Written demands may also be made for you to produce copies of (or signed authorizations for) such things as tax and medical records, your Social Security number, driving records, and other personal information.

Failure to comply with discovery demands or court orders is frowned on in all jurisdictions and can result in harsh penalties. Comply with all your attorney's requests for documents or appearances to avoid court-imposed penalties.

The defendant's independent medical examination

Because a defendant is being sued for a large sum of money in most cases, the defense has the right to have the plaintiff examined by one or more medical specialists, who prepare reports for defense counsel. These examinations enable the defense experts to evaluate the plaintiff and determine whether the condition is as bad as claimed and whether the incident in question is at fault.

You can and must help yourself during the defendant's physical examination by making sure that you're clear about what's bothering you and when you're in pain. Defendants' doctors take advantage of answers like "I feel alright" or "I don't always have pain" to imply that the plaintiffs injuries aren't that severe or don't exist at all. People hate to grumble about sickness, pain, and depression because they don't want to be perceived as complainers. The defendant's physical examination isn't the place for such concerns because it's your opportunity to let the defendant know just how badly you're injured. You can do this at your deposition to some extent, but the physical is the place to be very clear about it.

Avoid chitchat while you're being examined; these doctors are experts at gaining your confidence so they can ask you about the accident and other matters that have nothing to do with the examination but which may damage your credibility with respect to other facts about the case. Be honest; you only hurt your case if a jury thinks you tried to make it appear as if your injuries were more serious by exaggerating your symptoms. Examining doctors work for and are paid by the insurance companies and aren't there to help your case in the least.

Running Through the Stages of a Trial

Sooner or later, if your case doesn't settle, you'll proceed to trial, and at that point more than any other, you'll truly understand the importance of having retained a good, experienced plaintiff's personal injury attorney. Because most cases are settled or dismissed before a trial ever takes place, only the more difficult cases, or those where a settlement isn't possible, ever get to be presented to a jury. If your attorney isn't a seasoned trial lawyer, the end of your case can be swift and ugly.

Jury selection

The first order of business is jury selection. Each side (or the court in some jurisdictions) asks prospective jurors questions in order to determine whether the jurors can be fair and impartial and follow the law as told to them by the judge. Attorneys refer to this process as the *voir dire*.

Each side is permitted to challenge any juror *for cause* if the juror can't be fair. Each side also has a limited number of *peremptory* challenges to remove jurors the attorneys believe aren't sympathetic to their side. Seasoned, skillful trial attorneys use the *voir dire* process to have potentially unfavorable jurors removed from consideration in your case.

A *bench* (or non-jury) trial is one where only the judge decides the entire case after hearing the evidence. One way a bench trial occurs in a civil case is when both sides agree to waive a jury. The other way is when state law doesn't permit a jury. This occurs most often where a state, or one of its municipalities, is the defendant, or where the case is brought against the federal government under the Federal Tort Claims Act.

Opening statements

After the jury members are selected, they're sworn in, and the trial begins. The court usually gives some preliminary instructions to the jury and then each side usually gives its *opening statement*. The opening is the first opportunity each party has to tell the jury about its version of the case in some detail. Although what the attorneys say isn't evidence, many skilled lawyers believe that a powerful, coherent, and believable opening statement can win a case before any evidence is heard.

The plaintiff's case

The first part of the trial is the *plaintiff's case,* wherein the injured party is required to offer sufficient evidence to permit the claim to be decided by the jury; the burden of proof is on the plaintiff to make her case. The plaintiff's attorney calls witnesses and offers any relevant documents, records, photographs, reports, and other evidence in support of the injured party's case. You, as the plaintiff, testify at this stage of the trial. Your attorney questions you *(direct examination)* and the defendant's attorney questions you during *cross-examination.*

When you testify, you're asked about the incident in great detail, and you have to reconcile your testimony with any prior statement you may have made to witnesses or at your own deposition. You're questioned about your injuries and what effect they've had on your life and employment. In essence, you're responsible for convincing the jury members that they should find in your favor and award you a significant amount of money to compensate you for what happened.

Testifying at a trial requires you to remain calm and to be as forthright as possible. Use this opportunity to tell your story to a jury in person. Although this experience is strange for most people, you're prepared for it by your attorney, who also is allowed to object to improper questions from the defendant's attorney.

Certainly, you may have other witnesses and evidence on your behalf, but jurors always want to see the parties themselves in order to weigh the merits of the case.

The jury carefully watches you at all times — on and off the witness stand. Don't discuss anything about your case anywhere in the courthouse or do anything that makes you appear to be less than serious about your case or less injured than you claim to be.

Summations

After the plaintiff *rests* (completes his case), the defense is given the opportunity to present its own case by presenting evidence and calling witnesses. Unlike the plaintiff, who must prove his case by credible evidence, a defendant has no duty or obligation to offer any evidence at all. A defendant may choose to rest without calling any witnesses or introducing any proof of his own if he believes the plaintiff has failed to prove a case. Of course, doing so is a risky proposition for a defendant because the only evidence the jury (and court) then has is what was offered by the plaintiff. Accordingly, in most cases the defendant produces witnesses and offers other evidence tending to disprove the plaintiff's claims.

After both sides rest, the attorneys address the jury directly for the final time in their *summations*. During summations, attorneys tell the jury what they believe the evidence proves and what reasonable inferences flow from the testimony that was presented. Although anything an attorney tells the jury during summation is not to be considered as evidence, attorneys are given great leeway provided their remarks are "fair comment" on the evidence offered at trial.

If the jury is still undecided by the time summations are heard, an attorney who can present a powerful, coherent, and believable closing argument can often win the case on the summation alone. Often, an attorney can get jurors to change their minds during summation if he presents a believable theory of the case that interprets the evidence in a light favorable to his client.

After summations, the court *charges* the jury with all the applicable law they need to decide the case. The jury must accept the law as it's given to them by the court. They're free, however, to weigh the evidence as they see fit because the jurors are the exclusive and sole judges of fact. The court decides all questions of law, and the jury decides all questions of fact.

The verdict

After the jury has deliberated as long as necessary to reach an agreement, they return to the courtroom with their verdict. The verdict usually takes the form of questions that the jury answers in writing. The jury may be polled by the attorneys or the court to be certain the verdict has been recorded correctly.

Each side is entitled to make arguments to the court as to why the verdict is or isn't correct. These arguments are called *motions,* and after the court rules on these motions, the trial is over.

Although in a criminal case all 12 jurors must agree on a verdict in order to find the defendant guilty of a crime, many states now use juries of only six people in civil cases and some even permit verdicts to be less than unanimous as long as five of the six jurors agree.

Apportioning liability

Before awarding damages, a jury must decide in what percentage to assign blame for an accident. This area is where the laws vary widely from state to state.

Apportionment of liability refers to the determination by a jury (or the court in a non-jury case) of the percentage of fault attributable to each party. Fault may be apportioned between the defendants as well as between the plaintiff and the defendant or defendants. Chapter 3 gives you the details on apportioning liability.

The appeal

Although trials determine the outcome of a case insofar as a jury verdict is concerned, one side or the other often opts to have an appellate court review the trial in order to determine whether any errors were made that deprived one side of a fair trial or that require a new trial or some other action by the appellate court. Only after all appeals are exhausted is a case truly over.

Most jurisdictions permit *interlocutory appeals,* which occur while a case is being litigated and before a final verdict is rendered after a trial. Thus, many discovery orders, motions to dismiss, and other types of non-final determinations may be reviewed by an appellate court while a case is ongoing.

Every jurisdiction has at least two levels of appellate courts:

- An intermediate (or first) level hears most appeals.
- A second level, which is usually the highest court in the state, hears a more limited number of appeals and usually has strict rules for the type of appeals that it considers.

Sometimes, a state appeal finds its way into federal court for a final review, but such situations are very rare and only occur under extremely limited situations.

Avoiding a Trial with Settlements

Settlements can happen at any time and most cases are settled before trial. The important thing to remember is that greediness never pays off. Many plaintiffs turn down generous settlements hoping for an even larger verdict only to have the jury award far less than the settlement offer. Defendants, too, make the same mistake by refusing to increase an offer only slightly in order to save some money for the insurance company only to have the jury award far more than even the plaintiff wanted to settle the case. Unfortunately, these examples happen literally every day. Listen to your attorney's advice about whether you should accept an offer.

Structured settlements

Sometimes settlements are structured to pay out proceeds over time. Such settlements are often used in cases involving infants (especially those suffering catastrophic injuries such as brain damage). In this way, the child's medical and living expenses can be provided far into the future, even after the parents are no longer available to manage and support the child.

The settlement is determined in *present value,* that is, its worth in current dollars, although the actual payout is always significantly more by the time the structure period ends. One of the benefits of a structured settlement is that the interest paid through such a settlement isn't taxable if the settlement itself wasn't taxable. Another major benefit is that structured settlements are almost always written using life insurance (as opposed to casualty insurance) companies. Life insurance companies are highly regulated by the states and are more conservative than casualty companies as to the nature of their investments.

If you receive a substantial settlement, some, if not all of it, may find its way into the stock or mutual fund market. If recent history is a guide, much of your money may be lost, and the life care your attorney fought so hard to ensure for you or your loved ones will be gone. The ramifications are dire. Further, as soon as your friends and relatives hear that you came into money, they'll crawl out of the woodwork with all sorts of investment ideas and personal needs. If your money is placed in a structured settlement, you have access only to the payouts provided for in the structure and therefore a good excuse for fending them off.

Aggregate settlements

Aggregate settlements may occur in class actions and mass tort litigation. An *aggregate settlement* is a fund set aside to settle a number of claims. This fund can range from a limited amount of money allocated to a few plaintiffs to a huge sum allocated to thousands of plaintiffs or claimants. The proceeds of an aggregate settlement may be overseen by a court-appointed administrator, or Special Master, or by some other individual sanctioned by the court.

Insurance Considerations

Defendants sometimes have no insurance or maintain only a limited amount of coverage. In such cases, you may not have any assets to collect from, or the amount you may have access is inadequate to compensate you for all your damages. Sometimes this is the luck of the draw, and that's why you should always listen to your attorney's advice about when a settlement is wise.

You don't want to run up huge expenses and costs to litigate a case where your recovery is limited. Likewise, chasing a defendant for personal assets is often a useless quest that costs more than the recovery you ultimately obtain. Generally speaking, if a party has assets, they usually protect themselves with sufficient insurance.

Finally, all insurance policies aren't created equal. Policy limits vary widely as do types of coverage. Some policies pay up to certain limits "per occurrence" meaning there is a limit that applies to each accident even though the total coverage may be greater. Accordingly, if five people are injured in an accident, the insurance company allocates only a portion of the available coverage to each plaintiff.

Aggregate policies (usually held by companies or professionals) may have high limits, but as each claim is paid out, the amount available as coverage decreases. As a result, the first claim of the year may have a large amount of coverage to draw upon, while a claim coming late in the year may only have a small amount of coverage remaining. Because such policies must last for the entire policy period in order to protect the policy holder as much as possible, insurance companies are more inclined to always hold back a certain amount of coverage even in serious cases.

Chapter 3

Understanding Statutes of Limitations

*W*ine gets better with age; lawsuits do not. In fact, every lawsuit is subject to one or more "statutes of limitations." Wait too long to commence your lawsuit and you're out of luck forever, regardless of how great a case you may have had. This chapter takes you through the important details about meeting these critical time requirements.

Defining Statutes of Limitation

Statutes of limitations dictate how long you have to file a lawsuit. In the case of personal injury litigation, the type of case, the type of defendant (private, state, municipal, federal, and so on), and the state the injury occurred in are some of the factors used to determine the length of time you have to file a lawsuit. The upcoming section, "Identifying the Factors That Drive the Statutes," tells you more about these considerations.

For example, a case against a New York municipality has a much shorter statute of limitations than one brought against a private defendant, and a medical malpractice case has a shorter statute of limitations than one based on an automobile accident.

A statute of a different flavor: Statutes of repose

A *statute of repose* (SOR) is very different from a statute of limitations. SORs usually apply in products liability cases and are designed to limit the exposure of manufacturers and sellers. They're enforced more strictly and can't be tolled like a statute of limitation.

SORs currently are being applied more often in medical malpractice cases. A statute of repose begins to run from some specified time or event (the date a product is purchased, for example) regardless of whether any claim has accrued or any injury has occurred. Thus, an SOR may actually bar claims before they accrue and is designed to prevent plaintiffs from sleeping on their legal rights to the detriment of a defendant.

SORs in product liability cases focus on the age of a product, rather than on the date of the plaintiff's injury. The repose period serves as an absolute barrier that prevents a plaintiff's right of action. In other words, the end of the period of repose has the effect of preventing any action from ever arising. By way of an example, a common statute of repose is ten years from the date the product is sold or a construction project completed instead of on the date an injury occurred or the date the cause of the injury is discovered.

Different statutes of limitations also apply to certain types of federal cases or lawsuits against the federal government.

Often, more than one statute of limitations may apply in the same case. For example, you may be involved in an automobile accident with a municipal garbage truck or bus and a private car. Each defendant, however, is subject to a different statute of limitations. Also, in many states, different statutes of limitations exist for wrongful death and negligence cases. Thus, an injury that causes death following a period of pain and suffering may be governed by two different statutes of limitations.

To further complicate matters, certain factors may stop the statute of limitations in a certain case from running. A *toll* is a legal reason why a statute of limitations is suspended or extended. The toll may be in effect for a limited period of time, based on the circumstances in a specific case.

Tolls may include one or more of the following:

- Infancy or mental incompetence of the plaintiff

- Absence of the defendant from the state

- Continuous treatment by a professional

   Continuous treatment means any additional treatment or care by a medical professional or services by another professional (attorney, accountant, broker, and so on) that involves the same matter in which the malpractice occurred. Thus, post-operative care by a surgeon would extend the statute of limitations for malpractice committed during the surgery itself.

- Inability to discover an injury because it has not yet revealed itself or because the plaintiff is unaware that the condition he is suffering from was caused by the defendant's negligent act

- Fraudulent concealment of wrongdoing by the defendant

- Death of the plaintiff or the defendant

In addition, an *equitable toll* (a toll that is dictated by fairness) requires a court to determine whether facts and circumstances warrant stopping a statute of limitations. The court may grant an equitable toll when the defendant engaged in conduct that the plaintiff relied on in not timely filing their case (accepting a settlement check from the defendant on the eve of the statute of limitations only to have the check "bounce" after the statute of limitations expires). Equitable toll may also occur where the defendant engaged in conduct where the plaintiff couldn't timely identify the proper party but where that party was aware of the claim (the defendant was using an alias, or concealing the real identity of his business, such as a corporation or partnership, by operating it under a ficticious name that has no legal status — usually referred to as "doing business as").

Because so many factors play into a case's statute of limitations, you must consult with a qualified attorney in the applicable jurisdiction as soon as possible. Only an attorney who's thoroughly familiar with a particular jurisdiction can give you the advice you need to protect your rights from being extinguished by a statute of limitations. All too often, an injured person's claim is lost forever because he waited too long in retaining an attorney.

For examples of statutes of limitations, turn to Appendix A. (You can find more detailed information at `www.statutes-of-limitations.com`).

Identifying the Factors That Drive the Statutes

In determining the proper statute of limitations, your attorney considers numerous factors. She takes into consideration the answers to questions such as

- **Was the conduct involved intentional or negligent?** Intentional acts (also called *torts*) that cause injury, like libel, slander, assault, battery, and malicious prosecution usually have much shorter statutes of limitations than torts involving negligent conduct on the part of the defendant.

- **Will the claim be based on medical malpractice?** Over the past several years, most jurisdictions have substantially shortened the statutes of limitations applicable to medical malpractice without making similar changes for cases involving other types of professional malpractice. Thus, in the very same jurisdiction, claims against attorneys, accountants, architects, or even some other types of health professionals might have longer statutes of limitations than do claims against medical doctors, dentists, or hospitals.

- **Does the case involve an allegedly defective product?** Many variations apply to such cases, and statutes of limitations may also depend on how old the product is or how long the defect existed.

- **Was the discovery of the injury delayed?** Often, injuries caused by toxic substances, defective drugs, defective medical devices, and medical malpractice take months or even years to manifest themselves. Most (but not all) states now make allowances for such situations by using a *discovery rule,* which provides additional time for filing a lawsuit in cases where the damage doesn't immediately become apparent, but don't count on it.

Err on the side of caution: Seek medical and legal advice at the first sign of a possible injury. Never rely on a discovery rule as some kind of automatic toll that allows you additional time to begin a lawsuit.

✔ **Does the case involve a governmental body or agency?** The government, at all levels invariably receives extraordinary protection from being sued. This protection often means much shorter statute of limitations than those applicable to non-governmental defendants or complete immunity from certain types of lawsuits and even from punitive damage awards. Because such different rules apply in cases involving governmental bodies and because timing is even more critical when such entities are involved, seek legal advice from an attorney immediately. In these cases, even a short delay may result in your case being lost forever.

✔ **Does the claim involve a charitable organization?** In some states, charitable organizations still enjoy immunity from suit. In others, that immunity has been abolished. And in some jurisdictions, immunity applies to certain types of cases and not to others.

✔ **Is the plaintiff an infant or suffering from some type of disability?** Most jurisdictions recognize certain disabilities (infancy, mental illness, military service for example) as reasons to toll (suspend) statutes of limitations to some degree. This is because the actual plaintiff is unable to protect his rights as a result of the disability; however, the rules with respect to disabilities vary widely from state to state.

✔ **Is the defendant unavailable?** If the defendant is absent from the state, maybe because he's a member of the active armed forces or is incarcerated, a toll may apply, but each municipality has unique rules in this regard.

✔ **In what jurisdiction is the action brought?** Each state, as well as Puerto Rico, Washington, D.C., and the U.S. Virgin Islands, has its own specific statutes of limitations, and these statutes vary widely. Different tolls and rules also exist within municipalities in every jurisdiction. In addition, entirely separate statutes of limitations govern actions under federal law and against entities of the federal government.

- ✓ **Does the case involve a death?** A wrongful death case differs from the traditional personal injury negligence case in that wrongful death cases are created by statute (since they didn't exist at common law) and belong to the estate of the deceased person. The applicable statute of limitations (as well as damages recoverable) varies greatly in each jurisdiction.

Chapter 4

Measuring Damages: What Are You Entitled To?

Regardless of how negligent a defendant might be, no personal injury case exists without provable *damages* (physical or psychological injury, lost earnings, medical expenses, and so on). Imagine, for example, that you're eating in a restaurant and discover a large shard of glass in your spaghetti just before you are about to place it in your mouth. The restaurant is clearly negligent, but you have no case because you haven't suffered damages. Should you bite into the glass and cut your mouth, however, you do have a case because you have suffered measurable damages. A plaintiff always needs to prove some degree of damages to be successful.

Understanding Compensatory Damages

A very important element of any personal injury or wrongful death case is the amount of damages the plaintiff is entitled to recover. *Compensatory damages* usually fall into two broad categories:

- ✓ **Pain and suffering,** which includes past and present pain and suffering and its component parts, such as scars, deformities, complete or partial loss of a bodily function or organ, physical limitations, pain, loss of enjoyment of life (this is the value placed on the loss of those things that make life rewarding and enjoyable).

- ✓ **Special damages,** meaning past and future monetary losses — earnings, pensions, benefits, and so on — or expenses incurred, such as medical bills, pharmaceutical expenses, equipment rental, and travel expenses

Compensatory damages for conscious pain and suffering are the most difficult to place a value on because no two people or injuries are ever exactly the same. Pain and suffering includes any emotional, psychological, or psychiatric aspect of the plaintiff's injuries which, in some cases can be quite significant, and it includes the more challenging to evaluate component of "loss of enjoyment of life."

The jury is usually asked to break its award for conscious pain and suffering into

- ✓ **Past:** From the date of the occurrence until the date of the verdict

- ✓ **Future:** From the date of the verdict until a definite date set by the court or state law — ten years, for example — or for the duration of the plaintiff's life expectancy calculated by actuaries

Another form of compensatory damages is awarded to a spouse or a parent as part of a derivative claim that they have for the loss of services of a spouse or child. As a result of decades of awards and government studies, economists can estimate the cost of replacing the services rendered by a mother, for example, in terms of cooking, cleaning, running a household, and rearing children.

Defining Wrongful Death Damages

If a parent is killed, many jurisdictions permit a jury to decide on the value to be placed on the loss of parental guidance to any children. If a spouse is killed, a jury may be able to make an award for the loss of *consortium* suffered by the surviving spouse. This award includes such things as loss of society (including sexual relations) and whatever activities the couple enjoyed together. This type of award also applies in non-death cases where injuries are severe and debilitating. Some states even allow emotional and other damages to the surviving party.

Special damages are somewhat easier to evaluate because they can be mathematically calculated on the basis of expert testimony from a professional economist or by simply adding up bills the plaintiff has had to pay, the outstanding bills, and the bills that will have to be paid in the future. The jury is asked to break down this aspect of the award into past and future components.

In addition to his physical injuries, the plaintiff may suffer damage to his property (car, house, apartment, boat, and so on). The jury is asked to make an award for the property damage suffered by the plaintiff based on expert testimony or through bills and receipts.

In a wrongful death action, the measure of damages has nothing to do with pain and suffering. Instead, the jury is asked to place a figure on the loss suffered to the decedent's (the deceased person) estate; the recoverable elements usually are governed by statute and vary from state to state. So while a pain and suffering cause of action belongs to the person who was injured, even if she died, any wrongful death claim belongs to the dead person's estate.

The estate sues in the name of the decedent's legal representative when the person died without a will; in cases where a will applies, the estate sues in the name of the will's executor or executrix. The damages awarded for personal injuries pass to the estate and are distributed in accordance with the decedent's will or the relevant statutes, while the wrongful death award is shared by the *distributees* (legally recognized survivors) of the decedent according to the formula applicable in the jurisdiction involved.

Getting a Grip on Punitive Damages

Punitive damages are designed to "punish" the defendant. Sometimes punitive damages are referred to as *smart damages* because they're intended to make defendants "smart" so they don't engage in the same type of conduct in the future. Punitive damages suits arise when a defendant's conduct was so reckless that it amounted to willful disregard of the consequences. Intentional conduct fits this definition as well (see Chapter 11 for more information on intentional torts). Thus, a car company that knows a certain model will explode when struck in the rear yet hides that fact from the public and markets the car anyway is liable for punitive damages.

In addition to punishing the defendant, punitive damages are meant to send a message to other potential defendants that such conduct won't be tolerated.

When determining damages, juries work to make sure the award actually has a punitive effect on the defendant and so consider the defendant's finances. Certainly a $10,000 punitive damage award would have no effect on a multibillion-dollar pharmaceutical company. There, an award of $150 million may be deemed more appropriate. However, to a company with a net worth of $25,000, a punitive damage award of $10,000 may be sufficient to make the point.

Caps and Court-Imposed Limits on Compensation

Several states have caps on the amount of compensatory damages that a jury may award in certain types of cases. These caps are specific limits placed on certain types of recoveries by the state legislature. In all states, however, the trial court and at least one level of appellate court has the jurisdiction to decrease or increase any portion of a special damages award if it's obviously incorrect or if it "shocks the conscience of the court." The court may also raise or lower a jury award if it deviates materially from reasonable compensation based on a comparison with similar cases. The bottom line is the same in every jurisdiction; however, courts always have the last say when a damage award is challenged as being either too high or too low.

Your attorney can research cases like yours to ensure that the trial or appellate court has records of damage awards in similar cases. This information also is relevant to settlement negotiations. Listen carefully to your attorney when he advises you about settlement offers and the "true value" of your case. People often have an unrealistic opinion of the value of their cases based on advice from relatives or friends or newspaper reports that tend to stress the amounts that people sue for, which is always an inflated figure, or the amount of a verdict, which does not take into consideration subsequent reductions by the trial or appellate courts.

Apportioning Liability

Apportionment of liability refers to the determination by a jury (or the court in a non-jury case) of the percentage of fault attributable to each party. Fault may be apportioned between the defendants as well as between the plaintiff and the defendant or defendants. Laws regarding apportionment of liability vary widely from state to state.

The upcoming sections run down methods for apportioning liability.

Contributory negligence

Contributory negligence refers to any degree of fault on the part of the plaintiff which bars the injured party from any recovery even if the defendant is at fault as well. Even a finding of as little as one-percent fault on the part of the plaintiff prevents him from recovering anything at all. Contributory negligence is a harsh and antiquated doctrine that still applies in some states but that's been abandoned in many jurisdictions in favor of comparatice negligence (see the next section).

Comparative negligence

Comparative negligence refers to culpable conduct by the injured party that usually reduces his recovery to some extent.

Different jurisdictions have different comparative negligence standards in terms of how and to what extent a plaintiff's culpable conduct affects his recovery. Some states allow a plaintiff to recover as little as one percent; even if the plaintiff is 99 percent at fault, he can still recover something. For example, if the damages awarded are $100,000, the plaintiff will receive $1,000. In other states, a modified comparative negligence rule applies and prevents a plaintiff from recovery if he's more than 50 percent responsible for an accident.

Addressing multiple defendants

In cases involving more than one defendant, the jury must decide the percentage of fault attributable to each defendant. The jury's findings affect the rights of the defendants to collect from one another but *not* the right of the plaintiff to collect all of his damages against any or all of the defendants.

Joint and several liability refers to the legal principle that any and all parties responsible for causing an injury are answerable for it. If a person is injured in a three-car collision in which each of the drivers is negligent, the law regards the drivers liable collectively as well as individually. The plaintiff may proceed to collect from any one or all of them.

If a defendant pays more than the percentage assigned to him by the jury, he may collect anything over his share from the other defendant or defendants. This rule enables the plaintiff to recover from the defendant with the greatest amsount of assets or insurance, while letting the individual defendants worry about collecting from one another if they pay more than their share of the damages.

In some states, a defendant is responsible for 100 percent of the damages if he's even one percent liable (assuming the plaintiff isn't partially responsible). In other states, a defendant is liable for all the damages only if he's 51 percent or more liable for the accident. If he's less than 51 percent responsible, he is required to pay the plaintiff only his specific share of the damages.

Some states allow defendants to prove that a third party, who wasn't sued, was fully or partially responsible for the plaintiff's damages. In those states, the jury may apportion fault against the non-party in order to diminish the defendant's liability. Because there are so many variations, you should discuss your state's rule with your attorney.

Acknowledging the Workers' Compensation twist

Workers' Compensation rules may prohibit you from suing certain parties that caused your injuries, such as your employer or a coworker; however, defendants you're unable to sue may be brought into the case because they're sued by the actual defendant in your case. This occurrence is commonly referred to as a *third-party impleader action*. For example, you may sue the general contractor for a building project, even though your employer (a sub-contractor) caused your accident. The general contractor may be able to sue your employer claiming he's been made to pay for your damages as a result of your employer's negligence. With few limitations not relevant here, you can bring a third-party impleader action whenever you believe that another party is responsible for all or part of your damages — even if you choose not to sue that other party.

A plaintiff's ability to collect all his damages depends on which rule applies in the jurisdiction where the lawsuit is brought.

Chapter 5

Handling Specific Accidents

In This Chapter

▶ Addressing injuries from motor vehicle accidents

▶ Dealing with an accident on somebody else's property

▶ Coping with injuries from construction accidents

▶ Taking the right steps when you're hurt

Although motor vehicle, premises, and construction accidents are quite different in nature, they share many similarities in terms of the steps you should take to protect your rights immediately following an incident. These accidents make up the bulk of individual lawsuits, and so we've grouped them here, providing a description of each and a list of steps you need to take if you're hurt in any of these situations.

Motor Vehicle Accidents

Accidents involving automobiles, trucks, buses, motorcycles, and other motor vehicles (construction equipment, for example) that use the roads and highways make up the largest percentage of personal injury and wrongful death cases in American courts. In fact, a motor vehicle accident occurs about every 10 seconds in the United States — about 9,000 accidents every day and approximately 3.2 million each year.

Because automobile accidents are so common and can happen to anyone at any time, knowing what to do when an accident occurs is extremely important. The upcoming section, "Reacting the Right Way to an Accident " gives you more tips for handling these accidents.

If anyone involved may have suffered an injury of any kind, call for medical assistance immediately. Even a relatively minor collision can lead to extremely serious injuries to the spine, head, or nervous system; these injuries don't fully manifest themselves for days, weeks, or even months after the accident. If you don't seek medical attention after an accident, proving later on that an injury was caused by that incident is much more difficult.

Gather as much information at the scene as possible. This info includes licensing, registration, and insurance information from the other drivers, as well as the names and contact information of any eyewitnesses, because they may leave the scene before the police arrive or be reluctant to give their names to police or investigators.

Seek an attorney with experience in motor vehicle accident litigation. Take special care to do so when the accident involves a bus, truck, or train, because these vehicles often operate under federal licensing standards and are regulated by federal agencies, which often conduct detailed investigations of any incident under their jurisdiction. Certain records of interstate truckers are preserved for only a short period of time. An experienced attorney knows these facts and immediately pursue this avenue of inquiry.

Classifying Premises Accidents

The term *premises accident* refers to an incident that occurs on property of any type. Such accidents may occur in residential or office buildings; in stores, restaurants, banks, theaters, or garages; on vacant land; on driveways; in elevators or on stairways; in parks or swimming pools; or in schools.

Premises cases may arise out of things such as improper snow removal, poor maintenance practices, faulty plumbing or electrical wiring, design defects, and so on.

Don't delay in seeking a law firm with a proven track record with respect to litigation involving premises accidents. Some property owners have surveillance cameras that may have captured the incident. These video files are only kept for a short period of time. Therefore, notice to preserve the video must be served immediately or the video evidence may be lost.

The most important characteristics of all successful premises cases are

- The nature of the condition that causes the accident

- Whether the property owner had actual or constructive notice of that condition. (*Actual notice* is any situation wherein a defendant is directly aware that a dangerous condition exists. *Constructive notice* is the inference that a defendant became aware of a dangerous or defective condition because of the passage of sufficient time so that, in the exercise of reasonable care, the condition should have been discovered by the defendant.)

- Whether the property owner was responsible for the creation of the condition

Two different types of eyewitnesses may take part in most premises cases:

- A *fact witness* saw the accident itself.

- A *notice witness* has knowledge of how long the condition existed or who may have created it.

Many situations may spur premises accident litigation, but you need to take a couple of universal steps when any premises accident occurs:

- **Obtain the name of the premises owner, the management company, and the tenant of the premises:** Often, that information is posted at the location or is available from employees like doormen, superintendents, and handymen.

- **Notify the premises owner, management company, or tenant immediately:** Always establish a record of the accident.

Getting help from the legal system

As a result of the high risks posed by construction work and the realization that construction workers are often at a disadvantage when it comes to protecting themselves, most states have passed laws specifically designed to provide added protection to people engaged in various kinds of construction work. These include the erection, demolition, renovation, and alteration of different types of structures; excavation work, window washing; work being done in open shaftways, work on elevated worksites or where cranes pose overhead dangers, hoists, or construction materials; and work regulated by federal or state safety regulations.

In some situations, strict liability is imposed on the owners and general contractors at a jobsite, meaning that they may be found liable for simply permitting the unsafe practice or condition to have existed and a worker's own negligence isn't to be considered.

Always call for medical assistance when involved in a premises accident. Doing so immediately creates a record of the location of the accident and connects the injury to the incident.

Construction Accidents

The construction industry is extremely dangerous: Workers are exposed to hazardous conditions on an ongoing basis during most major building, renovation, demolition, and excavation projects. Often, to save money or speed up the work, employers don't provide the type of safety equipment and devices required by law. Workers are also forced to work in unsafe conditions or with the wrong type of equipment (or defective equipment). These conditions leave workers in the position of having to risk injury or death in order to keep their jobs.

Workers, themselves, frequently add to the danger by not using available safety equipment or by not following instructions given to them by their employers. These actions aren't the result of a worker's desire to injure or kill himself but, rather, may be brought about by a belief that the safety devices (hardhats or reflective vests, for example) are unnecessary or because the devices (safety lines, harnesses, or guardrails, and so on) are cumbersome and restrict their movements. An element of peer pressure also exists at construction sites and discourages workers from using devices that are perceived to be signs of weakness.

In addition to the workers, pedestrians and others passing by may be injured or killed if the construction site hasn't been secured by proper safety equipment.

If you're injured at a construction site, call for medical help immediately. In more serious cases, one of the supervisors or foremen at the site calls for you; in less serious cases, workers are sometimes discouraged from seeking medical attention at the scene. Failing to call can be a serious mistake because many serious injuries start out as seemingly minor.

We see more and more incidences of shoddy construction site practices resulting in the injury and death of workers and civilians, including resulting from the defective equipment, such as cranes. Reports show a number of situations wherein construction companies have paid off municipal inspectors to ignore violations or to certify unsafe construction sites and equipment as having passed inspection. Massive construction cranes that collapse onto the street and nearby buildings have proven to be quite destructive in major cities.

Report any workplace accident immediately so that it can be investigated right away by trained construction site forensic experts.

Construction accident litigation can become complicated very quickly; an owner or general contractor sued by the plaintiff usually brings one or more subcontractors into the case. Quite often, these cases involve state and federal labor laws, building codes and regulations, and governmental agencies such as Occupational Safety & Health Administration (OSHA) and Workers' Compensation. For these reasons, immediately seek out a law firm with a proven track record in construction accident litigation.

Obtaining witnesses names as soon as possible after a construction accident is especially important because

- Construction workers tend to move from job to job after completing their particular work (excavation, steel erection, concrete, and so on).

- Construction workers are often known to their coworkers only by first names or nicknames and, as a result, are difficult to track down.

- Construction work progresses quickly, and the accident scene simply vanishes in a short time.

- Contractors and subcontractors come and go over the course of a project, and so pinning down exactly which ones were present on a given day is difficult.

- The construction industry has its own "code of silence" that discourages workers from cooperating in the investigation of an accident even if it involves a co-worker who's seriously injured or killed on the job.

Reacting the Right Way to an Accident

Obviously, no one retains an attorney *before* an accident occurs, so what you do on your own, or with the assistance of others, immediately after you're injured has a lot to do with whether your lawsuit succeeds or fails. If you're injured in an automobile, premises, or construction accident, take the following steps:

- **Always call the police.** Even minor accidents can cause serious injuries and significant property damage, and a police record of the accident is proof that it actually happened and who was involved. The police are trained to

    - Obtain all necessary information from each person involved, which reduces the likelihood of forgetting to obtain information or being given false information.

    - Properly secure the accident scene to prevent secondary collisions

    - Control those involved in the accident in order to avoid potentially violent confrontations

- • Contact the proper agencies to inspect the jobsite, issue violations, take photographs, or even shut down the project

- • Call for medical assistance

- • Make an official record of the accident that provides valuable evidence of the incident later in the case

✔ **Call for medical help.** If anyone involved may have suffered an injury of any kind, call for medical assistance immediately. If you don't seek medical care after an accident, proving later on that an injury was caused by that incident is more difficult.

✔ **Take photographs if you can.** Even photographs taken by using a cell phone or disposable camera can be invaluable. (You might want to keep an inexpensive disposable camera in your glove compartment; you never know when it might come in handy.) If you're involved in

- • **A motor vehicle accident:** Photographs of the people involved (including witnesses) and such things as skid marks (or the lack of skid marks), the position of the vehicles, damage to the vehicles, traffic signs and controls, and weather conditions, make it much more difficult for people to change their stories. Pictures also serve to refresh witnesses' recollections many months or years after an accident.

- • **A premises accident:** Documenting a premises accident as soon as possible is extremely important because the dangerous condition is often repaired soon after an incident occurs. The condition may also change with the weather, as is the case in accidents involving slips and falls on ice and snow. If possible, try to place in the picture something with known dimensions, like a coin (a quarter is best), dollar bill, or ruler in the picture so that you have a frame of reference to establish the size of the defect. Always include one or more long-range photographs of the defect or dangerous condition in order to establish that it is on the premises and that it was in a position that made it hazardous to people in the area.

- **A construction accident:** Obtain as many photographs as possible of the jobsite, the equipment involved, and any signs that identify the companies working there. Photographs are especially important in construction accident cases because the ongoing work quickly changes the accident scene forever.

✔ **Pay particular attention to physical conditions.** Make a note of (or photograph) any contributing actors to your accident. For example, if you're in a motor vehicle accident, note whether traffic control devices (stop signs, lights) are broken, missing, or obstructed. You can't count on the scene remaining the same by the time you go to trial, so having a record of the condition is critical to your case.

✔ **Take notes.** If no camera is available, make notes of anything else that seems relevant. (Keeping a pen and paper in your glove compartment is a good idea. Many cell phones also have a feature to make short audio recordings). Write down as much as you can remember about the accident. If you're in a construction accident, for example, pay particular attention to any safety violations, the manufacturer (and model) of any equipment involved and whether it was defective, and the names of any supervisory or safety personnel at the site.

✔ **Speak openly to the police and medical personnel.** Do not speak to anyone except the police and medical personnel at the scene. The police are obligated to investigate incidents and file reports, and they therefore need to obtain a full and correct account of what happened. Medical personnel need accurate information regarding the mechanics of the accident to determine what type of injury might be involved. Give your full cooperation and as much accurate information as possible to the first responders. Giving information to others, however, will not be to your advantage and will, in all likelihood, be to your disadvantage and, thus, should absolutely be avoided.

✔ **Obtain legal advice.** Do not delay in seeking out a law firm with a proven track record with respect to the type of litigation you're pursuing.

Chapter 6

Looking at Products Liability Cases

Any product has the potential to injure or kill if it's defectively designed or manufactured, or if it isn't accompanied by adequate warnings. This chapter takes you through the basics of handling a case based on injury from such a product.

Understanding Products Liability Cases

Each year defective products injure or kill thousands of people. For purposes of liability a product must be considered defective in one of three ways:

- **Defective design:** The product was built according to a faulty plan. A design defect means that *all* of the particular products are defective. (For example, a gas tank designed in a way that causes it to explode when struck from behind).

- **Manufacturing defect:** A product's defect resulted from a problem in the manufacturing process. Thus, even though the product's design may have been flawless, something went wrong with the way in which the particular item involved in the accident was manufactured. (For example, instead of a teapot's spout being welded, it's glued and therefore falls off when boiling water is poured through it.)

✔ **Inadequate warnings:** The manufacturer doesn't provide enough information for a consumer to use a product safely. (For example, a manufacturer of commercial meat grinders fails to warn users that operating the equipment in a particular manner, which could reasonably be expected, exposes the operator to having his hand pulled into the cutting blades.)

Children are especially vulnerable to being hurt or killed by poorly designed toys; common packaging items such as plastic bags; small parts on household products; toxic chemicals that do not come in child-proof containers; and defectively designed children's products such as car seats, highchairs, strollers, cribs and toys. Even TV stands that are top heavy and not properly anchored injure and kill many children each year.

Most states recognize that many common products are misused by consumers. If misuse was reasonably foreseeable to manufacturers, they may be held liable for failing to warn users.

Taking Action after Injury

When someone is injured or killed by a defective product, take the following steps to increase the chances of prevailing in a lawsuit:

✔ **Preserve the evidence.** Preserve the product in a safe, secure location where it won't be tampered with or destroyed. Keep all the parts regardless of their condition. If the product was packaged in multiples, keep the entire group. If it's a perishable product, keep it frozen or refrigerated. If the evidence is large (like a motor vehicle), arrange for it to be stored safely and securely. If evidence is going to be taken away or destroyed, inform your attorney immediately so that she can retain an expert to examine and test the product.

✔ **Take photographs.** Photograph the product, including any serial or model numbers and any other identifying information.

✔ **Save your receipts.** If you purchased the product, hang onto or try to dig up the sales receipt.

✔ **Save product literature.** Always keep assembly directions, instruction manuals, labels that identify the manufacturer or distributor, and any other type of literature that comes with a product. Often, products made in foreign countries don't have the manufacturer's name on the product itself but on the packaging, so keeping the packaging is important. If you have advertisements for the product, save those, too.

✔ **Register your products.** Fill out and mail any product warranty, registration, or other forms that identify you as the purchaser of the product.

✔ **Check Web sites for safety information.** Look for product information on Web sites maintained by consumer watchdog organizations, the Consumer Products Safety Commission (`www.spsc.gov`), the Food and Drug Administration (`www.fda.gov`), and other agencies and organizations. Law firms also can be good resources.

Our Web site, www.yourlawyer.com, lists many recalls as well as reports and stories of accidents involving many different products; the site also offers a free monthly newsletter for which you can register to receive information on product recalls, dangerous foreign products that may not be labeled correctly or manufactured up to U.S. standards, and other information that relates to dangerous or defective products.

✔ **Obtain medical attention.** Get prompt medial attention so you have a record of the care you need and the manner in which you were injured.

✔ **Obtain legal advice.** Find a law firm with a proven track record of product liability litigation. Product liability is a highly specialized type of litigation and requires a firm that can retain top experts to analyze or test the product upon being retained. Waiting to retain experts and doing the necessary preparation even before the lawsuit is started could doom the case to failure.

Retain only a law firm with the financial resources and personnel to properly handle a product liability case, which may cost over $100,000 in litigation-related expenses. The defense will invariably be handled by law firms that focus on product liability cases and are very well financed (by the manufacturer or its insurance company); the firms probably will have represented the manufacturer in cases involving the same or similar products and therefore will already be up to speed on the unique design, manufacturing, and warning issues. The plaintiff's attorney doesn't have that advantage and needs to be involved at the earliest opportunity.

✔ **Consider contacting your state's consumer protection agency.** Every state works to protect consumers from defective products, unscrupulous vendors, and other situations that could lead to personal injuries or financial loss. If you have a legitimate claim involving any consumer-related matter, always consider contacting the appropriate authority in your jurisdiction for information or assistance. Doing so is especially useful in situations that may not be significant enough to justify retaining an attorney. Appendix B provides a list of the appropriate consumer protection agency for each jurisdiction.

Chapter 7

Recognizing Defective Pharmaceutical Products

*P*rescription and non-prescription (over-the-counter or OTC) drugs are all man-made chemical compounds that become foreign substances when they're introduced into the human body. As a result, no prescription or OTC drug is 100 percent safe or free of side effects; these drugs are thus subject to the same types of defects that other consumer products may fall prey to: defective design, defective manufacture, and inadequate warnings.

Grasping the Risks of Pharmaceuticals

Some consumer advocates and watchdog organizations consider taking prescription or OTC drug to be much like playing Russian roulette. Although some drugs are safer, have better track records, and have less dangerous side effects than others, you still take some degree of risk when you take a drug.

Through the years, the human toll in injuries and death caused by dangerous prescription drugs has been enormous.

One estimate puts the annual number of deaths from adverse reactions to and side effects from prescription drugs in America at more than 100,000. Thus, you're six times more likely to die from an adverse reaction to a prescription drug than in a motor vehicle accident.

In addition, thousands of Americans are seriously injured or die from adverse reactions and side effects associated with common over-the-counter medications and so-called dietary supplements and herbal remedies. Infants, children, and adolescents are particularly vulnerable to serious, and often fatal, mishaps associated with accidental overdosing, over-medicating, and off-label prescribing.

Since the late 1990s, there has been a dramatic increase in the number of drugs that have had to be withdrawn from the market. Inadequate testing and rushing drugs to market are prime reasons for this phenomenon. In fact, between 1997 and the beginning of 2008, 24 prescription drugs as well as numerous over-the-counter products such as OTC cold remedies for infants and children have been withdrawn from the market.

Public Citizen, a consumer advocacy non-profit organization, recommends that you not use any pharmaceutical until it has been on the market for seven years — they call it their "seven year rule." This time period is likely enough for most of the most dangerous side effects that the pharmaceutical companies didn't disclose to the Food and Drug Administration to surface.

Protecting Yourself When You Use Pharmaceuticals

Based on the serious risks associated with prescription and OTC medications, you need to be proactive when you use any of these products. Here are some of the things you can do to protect yourself and to prepare for any potential lawsuit:

> ✔ **Always keep a copy of your prescriptions.** You can't recover damages unless you can prove that you actually took a drug. An actual prescription is very helpful in doing that. Today, all pharmacies are computerized and

have copies of your prescriptions stored electronically in their computer system. However, pharmacies go out of business and computer systems sometimes lose data, so your best bet is to keep a copy of your prescription with your other important medical information.

✔ **Keep your receipts.** Because defective OTC medications can result in very serious injuries or deaths, you want to be able to prove that you purchased the product — *before* your injury occurred.

✔ **Carefully read packaging and product labeling.** The packaging and inserts from any prescription or OTC medication should disclose the proper dosage, potential risks, adverse reactions, and known side effects. You can find critical information about when you should *not* take the medicine under the "contraindications" heading. For example, you may be advised not to take the medication if you have certain bodily conditions (pregnancy, heart disease, advanced HIV), with other specific medications, with certain foods, or while exposed to sunlight.

✔ **Do your homework.** Review online information regarding any medication, paying particular attention to FDA press releases, public interest groups — Public Citizen (`www.citizen.org`) or Consumer Reports (`www.consumerreports.org`), for example — legal Web sites (like ours, `www.yourlawyer.com`), and news stories.

Many older drugs are cheaper and have far better track records than newer versions, which have gained fast-track FDA approval without adequate long-term testing. Public Citizen recommends that you don't take any prescription drug until it has been on the market for seven years.

✔ **Be wary.** Many unscrupulous con artists and criminals think nothing of selling counterfeit, poisonous, expired, or stolen prescription and OTC medications. These products are very dangerous and can injure or kill you. They may look like the real thing, but most of the time a little checking reveals differences in the packaging or appearance of the bogus product when compared to the real one. Even medications manufactured in foreign countries pose hazards because of poor quality control or impure or contaminated ingredients. Internet purchases can also cause a problem because you have no knowledge of where the drugs came from or how old they are.

Under no circumstances should you ever self-medicate by purchasing drugs from any source other than a licensed pharmacist. Many programs run by the states (Healthy New York, for example) and by the drug companies themselves permit those who could not otherwise afford prescription drugs to obtain them at little or no cost.

✔ **Talk to your doctor.** Speak to your primary care physician or a specialist about any concerns you have. Do not discontinue any medication abruptly unless instructed to do so by your doctor, the FDA, or the manufacturer. Patients need to be carefully weaned off of many drugs to avoid further injury regardless of any risk they may pose.

Doctors receive perks and free samples from pharmaceutical companies who are promoting a new drug, and so you should not hesitate to ask questions. It would be nice to believe that doctors aren't influenced by such things, but studies have shown that new or more expensive medications are often prescribed in lieu of older and cheaper (and safer) alternatives because of these promotions. Since you are the patient, you should do your homework and be prepared to discuss other available drugs with your doctor. Doing so helps ensure you are prescribed the appropriate drug and not one that is the product of market hype.

✔ **Document any reactions you have to the drug.** Be sure to make a record of any adverse reactions or side effects you experience.

✔ **Seek medical attention.** Get medical help immediately for any potential problems since you took the medication. Even if you aren't certain whether you've suffered an injury, undergo a thorough examination or medical monitoring; many problems caused by dangerous drugs are identified only by sophisticated testing.

✔ **Obtain legal advice.** Seek out a law firm that has a well-established track record in pharmaceutical litigation. Because this is one of the most specialized areas of practice, you must be certain the law firm you select has the experience to litigate against some of the premiere defense firms in the world, which have unlimited financial backing from the pharmaceutical industry and their insurance companies.

Chapter 8

Litigating a Defective Medical Device Case

As science and medicine combine to create cutting-edge technological advances, the field of medical devices has grown by leaps and bounds. Unfortunately, these new devices are prone to the same defects and failures as any other consumer product or pharmaceutical. Consequently, medical device litigation has also evolved into a highly specialized area of personal injury law.

The FDA defines a *medical device* as any one of a number of instruments or other medical products intended for use in the diagnosis of disease or other conditions, or in the cure, mitigation, treatment, or prevention of disease or intended to affect the structure or any bodily function, and which does not achieve any of its primary intended purposes through chemical action within or on the body and which is not dependent upon being metabolized for the achievement of any of its primary intended purposes. (A full definition is found in the Federal Food, Drug, and Cosmetic Act, 21 U.S. Code §321 [h]).

Classifying Medical Devices

Medical devices are separated into three classifications that depend on the risk they pose:

- **Class I:** Devices that present minimal potential for harm to the user and are often simpler in design than Class II or Class III devices. Devices in this category are those whose failure or misuse is unlikely to result in serious consequences. Some examples include electronic thermometers, breast pumps, surgical microscopes, ultrasonic nebulizers, sphygmomanometers, surgical tables, surgical lights, temperature monitors, and aspirators.

- **Class II:** These devices are potentially more dangerous than those in Class I and require more careful monitoring and more sophisticated safety precautions, which may include specific labeling requirements, mandatory performance standards, and post-market surveillance. They are generally non-invasive and include many diagnostic instruments whose misuse, failure, or absence (with no replacement available) would have a significant impact on patient care but wouldn't likely cause direct, serious injury. Some examples include X-ray machines, powered wheelchairs, infusion pumps, surgical drapes, surgical needles, suture material, acupuncture needles, ECG, EEG, treadmills, ultrasound sensors, endoscopes, and surgical drills and saws.

- **Class III:** These are the devices that pose the potential for the most serious harm and for which insufficient information exists to assure safety and effectiveness solely through the general or special controls sufficient for Class I or Class II devices. Such devices need pre-market approval and a scientific review to ensure the device's safety and effectiveness.

  Examples of Class III devices, which require a premarket approval, include replacement heart valves, silicone gel-filled breast implants, implanted cerebral stimulators, implantable pacemaker pulse generators (defibrillators), anesthesia ventilators, anesthesia units, apnea monitors, auto transfusion units, invasive blood pressure units, fetal monitors, incubators, infusion pumps, and external pacemakers.

In recent years, a number of medical devices such as hip and knee replacements, surgical implants of various types, and implantable defibrillators and pacemakers have proven to be quite problematic, resulting in many serious injuries, deaths, and the need to replace defective devices.

Protecting Yourself When You Use a Medical Device

You may not have the option to choose whether a particular medical device is used, especially with respect to a Class I or Class II device. But when you're facing the possibility of a Class III device being implanted in your body, take certain steps to reduce your chances of injury or worse:

- **Do your homework.** Many sources provide information regarding medical devices, including informational Web sites, consumer watchdog organizations, legal Web sites that discuss litigation involving the particular device, and government agency Web sites. Take advantage of every source of information available before committing to a major surgical procedure, the replacement of a bodily part, or the implanting of a critical piece of technology.

  Articles are published in professional journals by surgeons documenting failures of medical devices sometimes years before the lay press or FDA are made aware. These articles are usually available online, sometimes for a small cost. However, you can almost always access a summary or abstract of the article at no cost, and you may be able to get the entire article at no cost through a public library or in a school library.

- **Ask questions.** Because the final decision with respect to the use of most Class III devices rests with the patient, you should be comfortable with that decision and should never be pressured into consenting to the procedure. Ask your doctor and the surgeon every question you want answered about the device as well as the procedure that will be used to implant it. Discuss such matters as

  - Risk

  - The recuperative period and rehabilitation

- The useful life of the device

- The need for future replacements

- The device's track record and failure rate

- The possibility to reverse the procedure
  (if applicable)

- Restrictions that the device will place on your
  normal activities

You do have choices. Make an informed decision. Put the same time into making the choice of which medical device should be inserted in your body as you do in deciding which automobile to purchase.

- ✔ **Find out about your doctor's or the surgeon's experience with the device.** A doctor or surgeon who has had extensive experience with a medical device is at a distinct advantage over one who has limited (or no) exposure to the device. However, some doctors are influenced by the manufacturers' marketing methods — trips to exotic places, fancy dinners, tangible gifts, and so on. Patients must do their homework because, as history tells us well, doctors have made bad choices in the past as to which medical device to use even though there was more than ample literature on the serious issues with that device. Nobody cares more about your health and safety than you. You are your own best advocate.

- ✔ **Speak with people who have personal experience with the device:** The Internet is a great place to find people and organizations willing to share information concerning good and bad experiences with every imaginable medical device. Don't ignore this valuable source of information. We maintain a Web site, www. injurytalk.com, where thousands of people come to discuss issues such as this.

- ✔ **If the device fails, seek medical and legal help.** If you decide to use the device or have it implanted, you must be prepared for the possibility that, as with any other product, it may fail or not perform as it is supposed to. In that situation, you should immediately obtain the medical attention you need to replace or repair the device, remove it, or reverse the procedure (if possible).

> Afterward (or even while medical attention is being arranged), seek an attorney or law firm with a proven track record with respect to medical device litigation. Do the same if a loved one dies after she begins using a medical device.

Understanding Preemption

The concept of preemption itself is a simple one and necessary to prevent any number of situations that would infringe on the power of the federal government or impede the orderly enforcement of regulations on a nationwide basis.

Preemption means that when there is a conflict between federal and state law on the same subject, the federal law preempts (or overrides) the state law. For example, individual states are preempted from imposing their own individual speed limits on interstate highways under federal control. Likewise, the states cannot pass laws regulating immigration or air travel, and they can't set a minimum wage lower than the one passed by Congress.

On February 20, 2008, the United States Supreme Court injected the idea of preemption into the field of medical device litigation in a way that defies logic and puts the public at the mercy of manufacturers. The ruling confers immunity from liability for injuries or deaths on certain medical device manufacturers after their products are approved by the FDA. Thus, even if experts conclude that a medical device was defectively designed, the mere fact that the FDA approved it may be enough to shield the manufacturer from any liability under state law. This includes the unfortunately frequent situations in which medical device manufacturers withhold critical internal safety information about their medical devices from the FDA.

In short, the ruling means that consumers harmed or killed by some defectively designed devices have no chance of obtaining compensation unless the device is manufactured improperly or not made to the specifications approved by the FDA. This area of the law is presently in flux. The ruling does not affect all medical devices, and some question exists about whether future court appeals will extend preemption to cover pharmaceutical products marketed with FDA approval.

Because of the Supreme Court's ruling, you, as the patient, must be all the more willing to do a thorough investigation before consenting to the use of any Class III medical device.

Chapter 9

Suing for Medical and Other Professional Malpractice

*W*hen a professional is negligent in some fashion, that negligence is referred to as malpractice. Some types of malpractice (legal, broker, and accounting) cause only monetary damages, while other types of malpractice (medical, hospital, and dental) can be responsible for not just monetary loss but physical injuries and deaths.

Glimpsing a Malpractice Lawsuit

Although malpractice cases have many similarities with other types of cases that seek money damages, they have significant differences that require attorneys and law firms with a proven track record of success in malpractice litigation.

Malpractice cases are far more expensive to litigate than most other types (exceptions are pharmaceutical, medical device, and some products liability cases) because they require extensive investigation and discovery as well as one or more highly qualified experts to support the plaintiff's claim. These experts must be able to convince a jury that the defendant "departed from good and accepted practice" in whatever discipline the defendant practices. The experts required in these cases are very expensive.

Despite the expense, you want to retain experts at the outset of your case. For one thing, you want to make sure you have a viable case. Also, an expert can guide the attorney, advising her about which documents and other items of discovery are available and what information she needs to obtain from the defendant to ensure the case is successful.

Attorneys who are well financed and who work with skilled experts regularly have a great advantage over law firms that are unable to afford these expenses, don't regularly work with such experts, or — worse yet — wait until the last minute to retain experts.

Further complicating malpractice cases is that they often involve injuries or damages that aren't readily apparent to the plaintiff. Because people understandably place their trust in professionals, they aren't quick to associate injuries or financial losses with negligence on the part of doctors, accountants, brokers, attorneys, and other professionals.

In cases of professional malpractice, most jurisdictions have rules that allow you to sue even after a statute of limitations has apparently run out if you are still being treated, represented, or serviced by the same doctor, lawyer, accountant, or other professional. Also, if the professional has kept his malpractice from you by fraud or deceit, most states permit you to sue after you discover the malpractice that was kept from you. Because each state has its own specific rules in this area, retaining a knowledgeable attorney as quickly as possible is very important.

Note: When a doctor prescribes the wrong drug or the wrong dosage of the right drug, or when a pharmacy dispenses the wrong drug or the wrong dosage, the resulting lawsuit will be for malpractice against the doctor or pharmacist — not against the drug company.

Finding Effective Ways to Protect Yourself

You can do a number of things to protect yourself and to preserve critical information whenever you deal with any type of professional:

- **Be diligent in selecting any professional.** Always review a professional's credentials and ask for recommendations from others, or from organizations associated with the profession involved. You should also interview any professional before hiring him or her.

- **Do your homework.** Check to see whether the professional has been sued for malpractice in the past. Many states now require such information to be made available to the public.

- **Ask questions.** Never be embarrassed to ask questions or to seek explanations concerning matters that you do not understand or that don't seem right to you. Remember, a professional is supposed to be working in your best interest and should always be willing to explain what is going on. Any reluctance or refusal to comply with your requests may be a sign that something is wrong and that you should pursue the matter further.

- **Seek a second opinion if necessary.** Although trust is an important aspect of anyone's relationship with a professional of any kind, getting a second opinion is a good way to build on that trust or to uncover problems before they become irreparable.

- **Enlist an agency to investigate impropriety.** If you suspect negligence or misconduct on the part of any kind of professional, you usually can find one or more government agencies or disciplinary bodies that will investigate complaints from members of the public. These include bar associations, medical societies, licensing agencies, departments of health, disciplinary committees, and other investigatory agencies. In the most serious cases, such as those involving fraud, sexual misconduct, or other illegal activity, law enforcement agencies, including the police, the district attorney, your state's attorney general and even the United States Attorney's Office may have jurisdiction to investigate and prosecute professionals.

✔ **Trust your instincts.** At the first sign of a problem, trust your instincts instead of ignoring the situation. Too often, professional malpractice claims are lost or seriously impaired because too much time passes or key evidence is lost. Consult a qualified attorney with whom you can thoroughly discuss your concerns. Malpractice is truly a situation where it's better to be safe than sorry.

✔ **Preserve important documents.** Always keep copies of any correspondence you have sent to or received from a professional. You should certainly ask for copies of any documents you have signed, such as medical records, medical reports, hospital records, consent forms, retainers, agreements, releases, or forms that have been filed on your behalf.

✔ **Obtain legal advice.** Professional malpractice is a very specialized area of the law requiring your attorney to have significant knowledge about the profession involved. Consider only law firms that have a proven track record of success in the particular kind of malpractice involved in your case.

In medical malpractice cases, especially, the earlier you retain a qualified (and well-financed) attorney, the sooner the appropriate steps can be taken to obtain your records, thereby reducing the chance that they will be tampered with or destroyed. Further, retaining an attorney right away allows for the early retention of a qualified expert to analyze those records and help prepare the case for trial.

Chapter 10

Recognizing Negligence and Abuse in Nursing Homes

Nursing homes have become big business as the baby boomer generation ages and the demands placed on the medical system to care for the elderly are becoming overwhelming. Unfortunately, a by-product of this massive increase in eldercare as an industry is the neglect and abuse of our most vulnerable citizens — who are usually our parents and grandparents. As a former head of the U.S. Department of Justice, Nursing Home Initiative, Marie-Therese Connolly, put it "Unlawful abuse and neglect is widespread, underreported, infrequently prosecuted and the cause of untold suffering, injury, illness and death."

After the decision is made to place a loved one in a nursing home, serious problems may arise that the family never anticipated. Inadequate or substandard care, negligent treatment, or criminal conduct by nursing home employees may add to the family's feelings of guilt, anxiety, and fatigue.

Fortunately, conditions can improve through many ways, you can avoid problems, or you can obtain legal help with these problems.

The problems related to substandard care and criminal conduct are on the rise and present a matter for concern throughout the country. The steady increasing number of deficiencies cited by various state Departments of Health is alarming, and The National Center for Elder Abuse has reported that neglect of our senior citizens' basic needs is the number one type of elder abuse. Physical abuse by caregivers ranks as the second most common form of elder mistreatment. Almost one million senior citizens are victimized each year.

Types of Intentional Abuse

Many types of intentional abuse exist in nursing home. Here are a few:

- Assault and/or battery
- Sexual assault and/or sexual battery or rape
- Verbal or emotional abuse
- Retaliation for making a complaint or filing a grievance
- Unreasonable physical restriction, or prolonged or continual deprivation of food or water
- Use of a physical or chemical restraint or psychotropic medication for any purpose not authorized by a physician

Spotting Typical Nursing Home Negligence

The following list consists of ways to spot negligence in nursing homes:

- Failure to assist in personal hygiene, or in providing adequate food, clothing or shelter

- Failure to provide medical care for physical and mental health needs

- Failure to protect from health and safety hazards

- Failure to prevent malnutrition or dehydration

- Over- or under-medication

- Failure to take reasonable precautions to prevent falls or other physical injuries

- Failure to answer emergency call lights

- Failure to turn residents in their beds (leading to dangerous and deadly bed/pressure sores)

- Failure to take residents to the toilet (leaving them in soiled garments or beds)

Being Proactive

Because many residents are unable to communicate the abuse or neglect they are being subjected to, family members and friends must be keenly aware of and take a proactive role in preventing these situations from happening.

Since nursing home residents have the right to take legal action against their nursing homes and to be compensated, it is important for a relative or friend to have a power of attorney, health proxy, or other appropriate legal document executed by the resident, if possible, so their rights can be properly protected.

If you believe, suspect, or know that a friend or loved one is being abused, mistreated, neglected, or otherwise negligently cared for at a nursing home, you have remedies. You may

- Go to the administrator or director of the home with your concerns.

- Take photographs of the resident and any signs of physical abuse or negligent care.

- ✔ Make a complaint to the appropriate agency in your city or state.

- ✔ Complain to the residents' advocate if one is assigned to the home.

- ✔ If a crime is involved, go to the appropriate law enforcement agency for the town, city, or state in which the facility is located.

Nursing home cases can be very complex. Sometimes the negligent care spans several years and many different nursing homes and hospitals. The medical records that must be reviewed by experienced nursing home attorneys, nurses, and experts are often voluminous. Consult a law firm that has a proven track record in nursing home litigation and which can effectively represent the rights of the resident and his or her family by pursuing all appropriate legal remedies, including monetary compensation.

Avoiding Litigation

In nursing home situations it is important to remember that, while litigation is always available when things go wrong, your goal should be to have your loved one receive the best care possible. Therefore, every avenue should be pursued, within the nursing home itself, to

- ✔ Determine if a problem actually exists or whether there is simply a misunderstanding;

- ✔ Take advantage of available administrative procedures set up by the nursing home to investigate and resolve complaints;

- ✔ Speak with other families whose relative is housed on the same floor (or in the same room), or has similar medical conditions, to determine if that person has suffered similar problems; and

- ✔ Keep an open mind until you have all of the facts or unless you have evidence of negligence or abuse.

Recognizing Signs of Abuse or Neglect

There are certain telltale signs to look for in determining if your loved one is being abused or neglected or is suffering from malnutrition or some other preventable or treatable condition. Check these out:

- Physical changes such as rapid or unexplained weight loss, sunken eyes, skin breaking down, hair thinning, lip and mouth paleness, cracks around mouth, and skin rashes or tears

- Injuries such as fractures, bruises, contusions, or lesions

- Emotional or psychological changes such as confusion, disorientation, depression, withdrawal, fear or anxiety, unexplained mood changes, or unexplained refusal or inability to communicate

- Signs of dehydration (that can lead to dangerously low blood pressure, which can generate strokes and heart attacks and can cause infections, kidney failure, uremic poisoning and death)

- Bedsores (also known as pressure sores, pressure ulcers, and decubitus ulcers)

  These ulcers and their complications claim the lives of many nursing home residents. They develop when the blood flow to raised parts of a largely immobile person's body areas is reduced or cutoff all together. They can also result from sitting for a prolonged period of time, thus they are often called pressure sores. Pressure sores can develop in several areas when a person is in bed and often result in significant pain and may require hospitalization. All too often, bedsores lead to fatal complications from infection.

- Room conditions such as urine and/or feces odor, lack of attention to the resident's personal hygiene

- Presence of unjustified chemical or physical restraints

Since nursing home residents are so dependant on around-the-clock care and supervision, every effort should be made to find a reputable facility and then to monitor the resident's condition to ensure that care continues.

Choosing the Right Nursing Home

After a determination is made that a loved one would be best off in a nursing home, there are several steps that should be taken in judging the quality of care provided by a facility. A visit should be made to the nursing home where you should speak with current residents and carefully observe their physical condition. You should observe their hygiene, physical condition, and their ability to converse. Do not limit your conversations and observations only to those residents the nursing home wants you to speak with or see.

Tour the entire facility taking notice of the smell of feces or urine. This might indicate that residents are not being attended to as quickly as they should be. During your tour, look to see that pitchers with fresh water are available to the residents. Note whether the aides are assisting the residents who are unable to do things for themselves, such as pour themselves a glass of water or walk to the bathroom. Ask detailed questions about the staffing levels for the different shifts, and how many of the staff are certified nursing assistants.

Visit the facility during the different shifts to see what the staffing levels are. Make observations as to how much time the aides spend with each resident, and how much food is actually eaten. Also check on the residents that are being fed in bed. Make sure that the trays are not just being left in front of them and that one of the aides is actually assisting them with their meal.

Inspect the dining facilities and observe a typical meal. Ask to see a meal plan. You might want to eat one of the meals yourself. It is also imperative that you speak with the family or friends of other residents in the home. Find out what their experiences have been with the home and its employees.

In addition to those observations that may be readily apparent there are other signs to look for which may be indicative of physical, verbal or emotional abuse to a resident of a nursing home. Take note if any resident appears to be emotionally upset or agitated, withdrawn or non-communicative, behaving strangely or is isolated from the other residents. These could all be telltale signs of problems at the facility.

The presence of bed sores on any resident is an objective indication of improper care since the nursing home staff has a responsibility to move or rotate the resident and make sure they do not sustain these highly preventable injuries which could progress into extremely serious conditions including death.

Available, at no cost, is a report that you might want to review issued by the Office of the Inspector General, Department of Health & Human Services entitled, Nursing Home Deficiency Trends and Survey and Certification Process Consistency, which can be found at `www.oig.hhs.gov/oei/reports/oei-02-01-00600.pdf`.

Chapter 11

The Special Circumstances of Intentional Torts

All cases we cover in this book have one thing in common: They are all based on unintentional, negligent acts by the defendants involved. In many situations, however, the defendant actually *intends* to commit the act that injures the plaintiff. Those cases involve *intentional torts,* and the law has specific rules for plaintiffs to follow that are quite different from those applicable to negligence cases. The differences are extremely important to understand in order to avoid critical mistakes.

Understanding Intentional Torts

Intentional torts include the following:

- ✔ **Battery:** Intentional touching, without consent, that causes injury

- ✔ **Assault:** Intentionally putting a person in fear of a battery

- **Lack of informed consent:** When a doctor performs a medical procedure or surgery for which the patient did not consent or would not have consented if the risks of the procedure had been fully explained.

- **Unlawful imprisonment:** Intentionally and wrongfully depriving a person of his or her freedom.

- **Malicious prosecution:** Intentionally and wrongfully pursuing a criminal action.

- **Abuse of process:** Improperly and intentionally using certain types of legal remedies to cause damage to another.

- **Libel:** Writing damaging defamatory remarks.

- **Slander:** Speaking damaging defamatory remarks.

- **Intentional infliction of emotional distress:** Purposely causing psychological harm to another.

Grasping Intentional Torts' Unique Characteristics

When analyzing intentional torts, there are some common threads that create potential problems for the plaintiff.

Statutes of limitations

In most jurisdictions, intentional torts are all governed by much shorter statutes of limitations periods. For example, in New York, if someone hits you with his car because he is negligent, you have three years to commence a lawsuit. If, however, someone drives his car into you on purpose, you only have one year in which to sue.

Why the statutes of limitations are significantly shorter for intentional torts in many states is the result of an antiquated view that, because you knew who committed an intentional act against you immediately, you didn't need a lengthy statute of limitations. Also, intentional torts existed before negligence in the legal system, so whatever statute of limitations intentional torts were originally given simply carried over after negligence came into existence.

Some states have attempted to deal with this problem by extending the statute of limitations for at least some, if not all, intentional torts.

Criminal cases and insurance

Unlike negligence, some intentional torts (battery, assault, false imprisonment, and malicious prosecution) are actually criminal in nature, which means that the defendant who caused the injury may be prosecuted by law enforcement for his actions. You therefore may not have immediate access to certain evidence or information that's part of the criminal investigation, and that may hamper your civil case for some time. Other intentional torts (libel, slander, abuse of process) are *not* criminal in nature and proceed much the same as negligence cases.

Probably the most troublesome aspect of an intentional tort, however, is that any insurance the defendant may have will not be available to pay for your damages. All insurance policies exclude coverage for intentional acts by the insured.

Attorneys sometimes attempt to create insurance coverage by referring to the case as a negligence action. They also try to extend the statute of limitations by doing the same thing. The courts are not taken in by this and have repeatedly held that there can be no such thing as "a negligent intentional tort." Thus, if someone throws a rock at your head and hits you, there is no way to change that intentional act into a negligent one in order to obtain insurance coverage or to get the benefit of the longer statute of limitations. Many attorneys have been sued for legal malpractice for making this very mistake.

If you're the victim of an intentional act that is also criminal in nature (battery, assault, false imprisonment, and malicious prosecution) report it to the police immediately. Do not think that by not reporting the event that you will somehow be able to claim the conduct of the defendant was negligent and not intentional.

When an intentional tort may include a negligence angle

When an individual commits an intentional tort, the way to gain the benefit of the longer negligence statute of limitations and possible insurance coverage has nothing to do with the individual who committed the wrongful act. Instead, it has to do with the employer of that person. Thus, if a security guard at a department store assaults you and locks you up in a back room for an hour for no legitimate reason, you can sue the store on the basis of a claim that it negligently hired or retained the guard. If you are able to prove that the store knew or should have known of the guard's violent personality, the store's insurance policy will kick in and you have a better chance of settling your case.

Whenever an injury or monetary damage is caused by an intentional act, you must immediately protect your rights by retaining a qualified attorney to represent you. Serious errors can be made by waiting too long or by assuming there will be insurance coverage for the damages. If the person who injured you did so in the course of his employment, you may be able to recover from the employer's insurance company. In any event, be aware that intentional torts do not follow the same rules as negligence cases and be guided accordingly.

Glossary

Accrual: The date on which a statute of limitations begins to run.

Actual notice: A situation wherein a defendant is actually aware that a dangerous condition exists.

Aggregate settlement: A fund set aside to settle a number of claims. The proceeds of an aggregate settlement may be allocated by a judge, a committee of attorneys for the claimants, an appointed administrator, or by some other individual sanctioned by the court.

Answer: The document a defendant serves on a plaintiff that responds to the claims made in the complaint.

Apportionment of liability: The determination by a jury (or the court in a non-jury case) of the percentage of fault attributable to each party.

Bill of particulars: A document prepared by the plaintiff in response to a demand from the defendant for a more detailed explanation of plaintiff's claims, theories of liability, injuries, and other damages alleged to have been suffered.

Cap: A limit on the amount that may be recovered in certain types of cases or against certain classes of defendants.

Civil action: A lawsuit for money damages or other relief as opposed to criminal penalties.

Class action: A lawsuit brought on behalf of an identifiable group of potential plaintiffs who have suffered damages as a result of a common injury (monetary or personal injury) caused by a defendant.

Collateral source payments: Any benefit or payment to the injured person that must be offset from any damages awarded to him for the same loss in order to prevent what would be considered a duplication of benefits. Such payments include Workers' Compensation benefits, disability benefits, and some medical insurance.

Comparative negligence: Negligence or culpable conduct on the part of the injured party that usually reduces his recovery to some extent.

Complaint: The document that gives a defendant specific information about why, where (in which court), and for how much she is being sued.

Constructive notice: The inference that a defendant became aware of a dangerous or defective condition when a sufficient length of time has passed so that, in the exercise of reasonable care, the condition should have been discovered.

Contingent fee retainer: The legal agreement between a client and his attorney in a personal injury case; the basic rule is that a client is not responsible for legal fee unless she actually collects money by way of a settlement, verdict, or judgment, and the fee is then based on a percentage of that recovery.

Contributory negligence: Negligence or culpable conduct on the part of the injured party which bars the injured party from any recovery regardless of the degree of the defendant's negligence; this harsh doctrine has been abandoned in almost all jurisdictions in favor of one or another version of comparative negligence.

Created condition (also referred to as *caused or created condition*): A dangerous or defective condition the defendant caused or created.

Defendant: The person or entity being sued.

Deposition (also referred to as an *examination before trial or EBT*): An opportunity for each side in a lawsuit to obtain sworn testimony from the opposition before the actual trial.

Disability: Some condition (like infancy, insanity, or incompetence) that the law recognizes as a basis for allowing a statute of limitations to be extended.

Discovery rule: The time that the condition in question is discovered or should have been discovered with the exercise of reasonable diligence which begins the statute of limitations.

Discovery: (also known as *disclosure*) The process by which each side is entitled to obtain copies of reports, photographs, records, and other documents, or to examine other types of evidence that's in the possession or control of the opposition.

Federal statute of limitations: A statute set by federal instead of state law to restrict the time period during which a lawsuit may commence in certain causes of action, such as those for securities fraud.

Foreign object: Something not intended to be left in the body that has been inserted and left during surgery or some other medical procedure; a surgical instrument left in someone's stomach is a foreign object while a prosthetic device, no matter how defective it might be, is not.

Fraud of defendant: Conduct by a defendant that is intended to conceal his negligence or willful conduct to prevent the plaintiff from discovering its true nature before the statute of limitations runs out.

Immunity: Exemption from lawsuits afforded in some states to certain entities, (such as municipalities, governmental bodies or agencies, and charitable organizations).

Intentional tort: Deliberate acts that cause injury.

Interrogatories: Written questions posed to a plantiff (or a defendant) that may take the place of a bill of particular or deposition in certain jurisdictions.

Joint and several liability: The legal principle that any and all parties responsible for causing an injury are answerable for it.

Jurisdiction: The location where an action is brought or litigated.

Lien: A legal claim on a property used as an assurance of future payment. In lawsuits, a lien is a sum of money owed by the plaintiff that must be paid back from any recovery the plaintiff receives.

Loss of enjoyment of life: An element of damages to be included as part of any award for pain and suffering rendered by a jury; the law's attempt to put a dollar amount on the value of life itself and not simply the pain and suffering caused by an injury.

Mass tort litigation: Cases in which one or more defendants are claimed to be responsible for injuries to large numbers of individuals; such cases would include most litigation involving defective prescription drugs, toxic materials, dangerous products, and large-scale, man-made disasters, such as airplane crashes and chemical plant explosions.

Municipality: A generic reference to any state, county, city, town, village, or other political subdivision; it also refers to any division, agency, commission, or other department operated by the state or by any of its political subdivisions.

Negligence: Unintentional acts that reasonable people would regard as careless or posing an unreasonable risk of harm to others.

No-fault insurance: A particular type of motor vehicle insurance coverage carried by the injured person that pays him regardless of whether he was responsible for an accident.

Notice of Claim: A specific notice that must be served on a municipality or other quasi-governmental entity before a lawsuit can commence.

Occurrence: The event that gives rise to a cause of action.

Pain and suffering: The physical and psychological elements of an injury, as opposed to purely monetary damages such as lost earnings and medical expenses.

Plaintiff: The person or entity suing or bringing a lawsuit.

Punitive (exemplary) damages: Damages awarded over and above simple compensatory damages and intended not to compensate the plaintiff but to punish the defendant for actions that are willful, wanton, reckless, or undertaken with utter disregard for their potential consequences.

Retainer: A legally enforceable agreement between an attorney and her client with respect to legal representation; see *contingent fee retainer* above.

Statute of limitations (SOL): The time by which an injured party must commence a lawsuit; unless there is some special circumstance, the SOL begins to run from the date of the occurrence that caused the injury.

Statute of repose (SOR): A deadline for bringing a lawsuit usually applied in products liability cases and designed to limit the exposure of manufacturers and sellers.

Structured settlement: Any settlement set up to pay out proceeds over a period of time.

Summons: The document that commences a civil action and gives a defendant notice that a law suit has been started.

Toll: A legal reason why a statute of limitations is suspended; tolls include infancy or mental incompetence of the plaintiff, the absence of the defendant from the state, continuous treatment by a professional, and inability to discover an injury.

Tort: A civil wrong that entitles the injured party to recover money damages from the responsible party; a tort may be intentional (like assault or libel) or negligent (as in medical malpractice or an accident).

Tortfeasor: The person or entity responsible for injuring the plaintiff in a civil action.

Toxic substance: Any material that has the potential to inflict injury through exposure or ingestion.

Umbrella coverage: An insurance policy that provides coverage over and above that provided by basic insurance such as automobile, fire, homeowners, and so on; one umbrella insurance policy might increase the overall coverage on many underlying policies.

Underinsured coverage: Additional automobile insurance coverage that pays benefits when the insurance carried by the party responsible for the injury is inadequate to pay for the damage caused to the plaintiff.

Uninsured coverage: Additional automobile insurance coverage that pays benefits when the person or entity causing the injury has no insurance.

Workers' Compensation: Insurance coverage provided by employers to insure their workers and provide benefits to them for work-related injuries regardless of whether the injury was caused by the negligence of the employee or a coworker.

Wrongful death: A cause of action for monetary loss to the estate of a person who dies as the result of the negligent or intentional act of another.

Appendix A

A multitude of exceptions and special circumstances arise in every jurisdiction, so don't use this appendix for anything other than illustrative purposes. ***Warning:*** Only an attorney licensed to practice in the relevant jurisdiction can render the legal service of advising on the applicable statute of limitations governing a specific case.

State	Negligence	Wrongful Death [2]	Products Liability [3]	Med. Malpractice [4]	Other Malpractice [5]	Intentional Torts [6]	Claims vs. Municipalities [7]
Alabama	2	2	2	2/4 SOR	2	2	Limited
Alaska	2	2	2	2	2	2	2
Arizona	2	2	2	2	2	1	180 days/1 year
Arkansas	3	3	3	2	3	1	Limited
California	2	2	2	3	1	1	6 months
Colorado	2	2	2	2	2	1	180 days/Limited
Connecticut	2/3 SOR	2	3/10 SOR	2/3 SOR	2	1	2
Delaware	2	2	2	2/3 SOR	2	2	Limited
D.C.	10	1	3	3	3	1	Limited
Florida	4	2	4	2	2	4	3 years/4 years
Georgia	2	2	2/5 SOR	2	2	2 or 1	1
Hawaii	2	2	2	2/6 SOR	2 or 6 legal	2	2
Idaho	2	2	2	2	2	2	2
Illinois	2	2	2/10 or 12 SOR	2	2/6 SOR	1 or 2	1
Indiana	2	2	2/10 SOR	2	2	2	270 days/2 years

State	Negligence	Wrongful Death [2]	Products Liability [3]	Med. Malpractice [4]	Other Malpractice [5]	Intentional Torts [6]	Claims vs. Municipalities [7]
Iowa	2	2	2	2	2	2	2years/2years
Kansas	2	2	2	2/4 SOR	2	1	2years/2years
Kentucky	2 or 1	2 or 1	1	1/5 SOR	1	1/5 SOR	1yr./1yr.
Louisiana	1	1	1	1/3 SOR	1/3 SOR	1	1
Maine	6	2	6	3	4	2	2
Maryland	3	3	3	5 or 3	3	1	Limited
Massachusetts	3	3	3	3/7 SOR	3	3	3
Michigan	3	3	3/10 SOR	2/6 SOR	2	1 or 2	Limited
Minnesota	6	3	4	2	2	2	6
Missouri	5	3 or 10	5	2	5	2	Limited
Mississippi	3	3	3	2/7 SOR	3	1	Limited
Missouri	5	3 or 10	5	2	5	2	Limited
Montana	3	3	3	3/5 SOR	3	2	6 months or 1 year
Nebraska	4	2	4/10 SOR	2	2	1	2
Nevada	2	2	4	4	4 or 2	2	2

(continued)

State	Negligence	Wrongful Death [2]	Products Liability [3]	Med. Malpractice [4]	Other Malpractice [5]	Intentional Torts [6]	Claims vs. Municipalities [7]
New Hampshire	3	3	3/12 SOR	3	3	3	3
New Jersey	2	2	2	2	2	1	90 days/6 months/ 2 years
New Mexico	3	3	3	3	3 or 4	3	Limited
New York	3	2	3	2.5	3	1	90 days/1year
N.Carolina	3/10 SOR	2	6	3/10 SOR	3/10 SOR	3 OR 1	2
N. Dakota	6	2	10 SOR	2/6 SOR	2/6 SOR	2	180 days/3 years
Ohio	2	2	2	1/4 SOR	1	1	2 years/Limited
Oklahoma	2	2	2	2	2	1	180 days after claim denied/Limited
Oregon	2	3	2	2/5 SOR	2	2	Limited
Pennsylvania	2	2	2	2	2	1 or 2	6 months/2 years
Puerto Rico	1	1	1	1	1	1	90 days/1 year
Rhode Island	3	3	3	3	3	1 or 3	1 year/3 year/Limited
S. Carolina	3	3	3	3/6 SOR	3	2	Limited
S. Dakota	3	3	3	2	3	2	Limited

State	Negligence	Wrongful Death [2]	Products Liability [3]	Med. Malpractice [4]	Other Malpractice [5]	Intentional Torts [6]	Claims vs. Municipalities [7]
Tennesse	1	1	1/6 or 10 SOR	1	1	6 months or 1 year	1
Texas	2	2	2	1/10 SOR	1/10 SOR	1	6 months/2 years
Utah	2	2	2	2	2	1	2
Vermont	3	2	3	3	3	3	Limited
Virgin Islands	2	2	2	2	2	2	Limited
Virginia	2	2	2	2	2	1	6 months/Limited
Washington	3	3	3	3/8 SOR	3	2	120 days/3 years
W. Virginia	2	2	2	2	2	2	Limited
Wisconsin	3	3	3	3/5 SOR	2	2	120 days/Limited
Wyoming	4	2	4	2	2	1	2 years for NOC then 1 year SOL from filing/Limited

1 — A thorough discussion of Statutes of Limitations (SOL) can be found herein at Chapter 2 and at `www.statutes-of-limitations.com`. For example, entries listed as 2/5 SOR, indicate a 2-year statute of limitations with a 5-year statute of repose. For a definition of terms, see the glossary.

2 — These actions belong to the estate of the decedent and are brought by the legal representative of the deceased. Be advised that there are many variations with respect to wrongful death actions across the country. Although most states measure the SOL from the date of death, some states utilize the "discovery rule" to permit wrongful death actions to be brought within the applicable discovery period from when you knew or should have known that the death was caused by a product, exposure or event. For example, Florida, has a statute (F.S.A. 768.20), which terminates (abates) any "personal injury" action brought or yet to be brought but permits "wrongful death" actions.

3 — Each state has different rules that affect these statutes of limitations or repose including rules as to the affect of "discovery" of the cause of the injury or death.

4 — Many states differentiate between medical, dental, and hospital malpractice cases and those involving other professionals.

5 — "Other" applies to professionals such as attorneys, accountants, architects, engineers and brokers.

6 — Intentional torts include such things as libel, slander, assault, battery, malicious prosecution, and false imprisonment. Some states have more than one statute of limitations depending on the specific tort involved.

7 — These cases usually require some type of Notice of Claim (NOC) to be served on the municipality before a lawsuit may be commenced. If there are two entries (ex. 180days/1yr.), the first number is for the filing of a Notice of Claim and the second number is the statute of limitations. Both must be timely satisfied. Also be aware that states listed as "Limited" permit either alternative procedures for making claims (such as through a specific administrative agency), limitations on the amount that may be recovered (either in a specific figure or up to the amount of insurance coverage), or with respect to which entities or employees may or may not be sued.

CONSULT WITH AN ATTORNEY REGARDING ALL LEGAL ISSUES INCLUDING NOTICE OF CLAIMS AND STATUTE OF LIMITATIONS

Appendix B

Consumer Protection Agencies by Jurisdiction

Alabama Office of Attorney General, Consumer Protection
www.ago.state.al.us/consumer.cfm
(334) 242-7334
(800) 392-5658 (toll-free in Alabama)

Alaska Office of Attorney General, Consumer Protection
www.law.state.ak.us/department/civil/consumer/
cpindex.html
(907) 465-2133
(907) 465-2075 (Fax)

Arizona Office of the Attorney General, Consumer Protection
www.azag.gov/
(602) 542-5763
(602) 542-5025 (Phoenix)
(602) 542-4085 (Fax)
(800) 352-8431 (toll-free in Arizona)

Arkansas Office of the Attorney General, Consumer Protection
www.arkansasag.gov/consumers_protection.html
(501) 682-2007
(800) 482-8982 (toll-free in Arkansas)

California Department of Consumer Affairs
www.dca.ca.gov/
(916) 445-1254
(800) 952-5210 (toll-free in California)

Colorado Office of the Attorney General, Consumer Protection
www.ago.state.co.us/contact_us.cfm.html
(303) 866-4500
(303) 866-5691 (Fax)

Connecticut Department of Consumer Protection
www.ct.gov/dcp/site/default.asp
(860) 713-6050
(800) 842-2649 (toll-free in Colorado)
(860) 713-7239 (Fax)

D.C. Office of the Attorney General,
Consumer Protection
http://occ.dc.gov/occ/site/default.asp
(202) 727-3400

Florida Office of the Attorney General,
Consumer Protection
http://myfloridalegal.com/consumer
(850) 414-3300
(866) 966-7226 (Fraud Hotline)

Georgia, Governor's Office of Consumer Affairs
http://consumer.georgia.gov/
(404) 651-8600
(800) 869-1123 (toll-free in Georgia)

Hawaii, Department of Commerce
and Consumer Affairs
www.hawaii.gov/dcca/
(808) 974-4000 (ext. 7-3222)

Idaho Office of the Attorney General,
Consumer Protection Unit
www2.state.id.us/ag/consumer/
(208) 334-2400
(208) 854-8071 (Fax)
(800) 432-3545 (toll-free in Idaho)

Illinois Consumer Fraud Bureau
www.ag.state.il.us/consumers/
(800) 386-5438 (Chicago)
(800) 243-0618 (Springfield)
(800) 243-0607 (Carbondale)
Spanish Language Toll-Free Hotline: (866) 310-8398

Indiana Office of the Attorney General,
Consumer Protection
www.in.gov/attorneygeneral/consumer/
(317) 232-6330
(800) 382-5516

Iowa Office of the Attorney General,
Consumer Protection
`www.state.ia.us/government/ag/consumer/index.`
`html`
(515) 281-5926
(515) 281-6771 (Fax)
(888) 777-4590

Kansas Office of the Attorney General,
Consumer Protection
`www.ksag.org/content/page/id/39`
(785) 296-3751
(785) 291-3699 (Fax)
(800) 432-2310 (toll-free in Kansas)

Kentucky Office of the Attorney General,
Consumer Protection
`http://ag.ky.gov/cp/`
(888) 432-9257

Louisiana Office of the Attorney General, Consumer
Protection
`www.ag.state.la.us` (Click the
"Consumer Complaints" link)
(225) 326-6465
(800) 351-4889 (toll-free in Louisiana)
(225) 326-6499 (Fax)

Maine Office of the Attorney General,
Consumer and Antitrust Division
`www.maine.gov/ag/consumer/index.shtml`
(207) 626-8840

Maryland Office of the Attorney General,
Consumer Protection
`www.oag.state.md.us/Consumer/index.htm`
(410) 528-8662 (Consumer Hotline)
(888) 743-0023

Massachusetts Office of the Attorney General, Consumer and
Antitrust Division
`www.ago.state.ma.us/sp.cfm?pageid=967`
(617) 727-8400 (Consumer Hotline)

Minnesota Office of the Attorney General,
Consumer Services Division
www.ag.state.mn.us
(651) 296-3353
(800) 657-3787 (toll-free in Minnesota)

Mississippi Office of the Attorney General:
Consumer Section
www.ago.state.ms.us/index.php/
sections/consumer
(800) 281-4418 (toll-free hotline)
(601) 359-4230
(601) 359-4231 (Fax)
(228) 386-4400 (Biloxi)

Missouri Office of the Attorney General,
Consumer Protection Division
www.ago.mo.gov/Consumer- Protection.htm
(800) 392-8222 (Consumer Protection Hotline)

Montana Attorney General, Consumer Protection
http://doj.mt.gov/consumer/
(406) 444-2026
(406) 444-3549

Nebraska Department of Justice, Consumer Protection
Division
www.ago.state.ne.us/
(402) 471-2682
(800) 727-6432 (toll-free in Nebraska)
En Espanol: (888) 850-7555

Nevada Office of the Attorney General,
Consumer Protection
http://ag.state.nv.us/org/bcp/bcp.htm
(702) 486-3420 (Las Vegas)
(775) 688-1818 (Reno)
(775) 684-1100 (Carson City)

New Hampshire Office of Attorney General, Consumer
Protection and Antitrust Bureau
http://doj.nh.gov/consumer/index.html
(603) 271-3658
(603) 271-2110 (Fax)

New Jersey Division of Consumer Affairs
www.state.nj.us/lps/ca/home.htm
(973) 504-6200 (Consumer Hotline)
(800) 242-5846 (toll-free in New Jersey)

New Mexico Office of Attorney General,
Consumer Protection Division
www.nmag.gov/office/ConsumerInfo/default.aspx
(800) 678-1508 (toll-free in New Mexico)
(505) 827-6000 (Santa Fe)
(505) 222-9000 (Albuquerque)
(505) 526-2280 (Las Cruces)

New York Office of the Attorney General, Bureau
of Consumer Frauds and Protection
www.oag.state.ny.us/consumer/consumer_issues
.html
(800) 771-7755 (Consumer Hotline)

North Carolina Office of the Attorney General, Consumer
Protection
www.ncdoj.com/consumerprotection/cp_about.jsp
(919) 716-6400
(877) 5-NO-SCAM (toll-free Consumer Protection Hotline)

North Dakota Office of the Attorney General, Consumer
Protection
www.ag.state.nd.us/CPAT/CPAT.htm
(701) 328-3404 (Consumer Hotline)
(800) 472-2600

Ohio Office of the Attorney General, Consumer Protection
http://agcares.ag.state.oh.us/public/landing
.aspx
(800) 282-0515

Oklahoma Office of the Attorney General, Consumer Practices
www.oag.state.ok.us/oagweb.nsf/Consumer!
OpenPage
(405) 521-3921 (Oklahoma City)
(918) 581-2885 (Tulsa)

Oregon Department of Justice, Financial Fraud Section
www.doj.state.or.us/finfraud/
(503) 378-4400 (Salem)

(503) 229-5576 (toll-free in Portland)
(877) 877-9392 (toll-free in Oregon)

Pennsylvania Office of Attorney General,
Bureau of Consumer Protection
www.attorneygeneral.gov/consumers.aspx
(717) 787-3391
(800) 441-2555 (Consumer Protection Hotline)

Puerto Rico Department of Justice, Consumer Protection
www.justicia.gobierno.pr/rs_template/v2/Ciudad/
(787) 763-1985 (San Juan)

Rhode Island Department of Attorney General,
Consumer Protection
www.riag.state.ri.us/civilcriminal/consumerpro-
tection.php
(401) 274-4400

South Carolina Department of Consumer Affairs
www.scconsumer.gov/
(803) 734-4200
(800) 922-1594 (toll-free in South Carolina)

South Dakota Office of the Attorney General,
Consumer Protection
www.state.sd.us/attorney/office/divisions/con-
sumer/default.asp
(605) 773-4400
(800) 300-1986 (South Dakota only)

Tennessee Office of Attorney General,
 Consumer Protection
www.state.tn.us/consumer/
(615) 741-2241

Texas Office of Attorney General,
 Consumer Protection
www.oag.state.tx.us/consumer/index.shtml
(800) 621-0508 (Consummer Fraud Hotline)

Utah Department of Commerce Division
of Consumer Protection
www.consumerprotection.utah.gov/
(801) 530-6601
(800) 721-SAFE

Vermont Office of the Attorney General,
Consumer Protection
www.atg.state.vt.us/display.php?smod=8
(802) 828-3171

Virgin Islands Department of Licensing
and Consumer Affairs
www.dlca.gov.vi/
(340) 773-2226 (St. Croix)
(340) 693-8036 (St. John)
(340) 774-3130 (St. Thomas)

Virginia Office of the Attorney General, Antitrust and
Consumer Litigation Section
www.oag.state.va.us/Consumer/index.html
(804) 786-2071

Washington Office of Attorney General, Consumer and
Business Fair Practices Division
www.atg.wa.gov/SafeguardingConsumers.aspx
(800) 551-4636 (toll-free in Washington)
(800) 692-5082
(206) 464-6811 (consumer line)

West Virginia Office of the Attorney General, Consumer
Protection
www.wvago.gov/consumers.cfm
(304) 558-2021 (Main Office)
(304) 558-8986 (Consumer Protection Anti-Trust Division)
(800) 368-8808 (toll-free consumer hotline)

Wisconsin Department of Justice, Consumer Protection
www.doj.state.wi.us/columns/index.asp
(608) 266-1221

Wyoming Office of the Attorney General,
Consumer Protection Division
http://attorneygeneral.state.wy.us/consumer.htm
(307) 777-7874
(800) 438-5799 (toll-free hotline)

Index

• *E* •

• *F* •

• *M* •

• *N* •

O